Visions in My Mind's Eye

a collection of poems

IRMAGARD ANCHANG LANGMIA

iUniverse, Inc.
Bloomington

Visions in My Mind's Eye
A Collection of Poems

iUniverse books may be ordered through booksellers or by contacting:

iUniverse
1663 Liberty Drive
Bloomington, IN 47403
www.iuniverse.com
1-800-Authors (1-800-288-4677)

ISBN: 978-1-4620-3640-0 (sc)
ISBN: 978-1-4620-3641-7 (e)
ISBN: 978-1-4620-3642-4 (dj)

Library of Congress Control Number: 2011912577

Printed in the United States of America

iUniverse rev. date: 10/31/2011

Acknowledgments

With special thanks to my mother,
Juliana Anchang, and in memory of
my dad, Dr. Joseph Anchang Ngongwikuo.

To my darling husband Dr. Kehbuma Langmia,
thanks for all the comments and advice.

To all my sisters and brothers namely - Jane, Concilia,
Charles, Innocent, Bernard, Pauly, and Jude, thanks for everything.

To my sons Brandon and Gabriel-Phil, thanks for
the fun we had while writing some of these poems.
It was awesome.

"No matter how vivid a memory you have of honeysuckle crowding a creek bed, it remains locked away from a reader until you deliver it into language. You have to use words to make a reader smell the honeysuckle or hear the cellophane crinkle on a package of crackers."

(Wallace and Boisseau 259)

Contents

Part III: Love and Relationships: A True Vision of Life

Part IV: Secular: A Vision of Routine Life

Part V: Politics and Relationships: A Vision of Reality that Questions Morality

Introduction

Dear Reader,

When I was a young child growing up in the small village of Bambui in the northwest region of Cameroon, my window to the world was very limited. My father was a student in the University of Edinburgh in Great Britain and later, at the University of Yaoundé in Cameroon, while my mother was a teacher at St Peter's, the Catholic elementary school in Bambui. I was raised with a very practical and unsophisticated lifestyle in a Catholic mission in my early years. Every morning, I usually stepped outside to the veranda of our red brick house to stare in awe and consternation at Mother Nature and listen amusingly yet curiously to the rhythmic quacks of parrots, eagles, swallows, hawks, egrets, and ostriches that perched on the eucalyptus treetops lining the edged lawns of the St. Peter's football field across the street.

Little did I know then that beyond Bambui, there was another world out there that comprised continents, nations, and people of all colors who travelled around the globe. However, I was only five years old then, gradually growing into a young child. But as I matured and blossomed into a young woman, as I traversed the Atlantic Ocean to explore the universe that lay beyond the territory of my birth, I reflected on my ignorance and the sophisticated nature of a world, which was totally foreign to me then.

Poetry, like the flow of a stream that gradually soaks into the ground to restart its generational process, has gradually seeped into my brain. I now find myself waking up nights with a sudden and forceful urgency of thought. When that happens, I scramble from my bed and pounce on my keyboard before these thoughts escape my mind. Honestly, in my college years, I was never enthusiastic about poetry. During my Yaoundé University years, the only time I found poetry exciting was when my English professor, the late Dr. Siga Asanga, demystified Okot P'Bitek's "Song of Lawino," a poem in which Lawino chastised her husband, Ocol, for abandoning traditional values and pursuing European ones. What was so obvious in my negative attitude about poetry was the fear of misinterpreting the poet's line of thought.

Yet, the question that arises is the following: Should a poem written by a poet be tied to a single interpretation, or should it be subject to multiple interpretations by the reader? Which interpretation is recommended for the student in the classroom who studies poetry? Whether the reader agrees or disagrees on this subject of single or multiple interpretations of a poem, the truth is that all depends on the curriculum demands within the system in which the teacher finds him or herself. It is for this reason that I now leave the reader with this ideological food for thought, highlighting my views on the diverse interpretations that poems are often subject to.

Poetic Style

The difference in poetic style
lies in the mindset of varieties
pen handled by assorted geniuses
of varying cultures.

Clustered in closets of multiple ideologies,
identical to individual talent, it is an exciting
breakthrough for poetic gluttons who cannot
but help intellectually—
consume,   *absorb,*
pause,   *then,*
   meditate.

So, read through the lines,
for the stanzas' highs and lows iterate my poetic
choices, be they conventional or otherwise;

  because,
a fresh stream of phobic ideologies
stringed in lettered words, then partitioned
and bottled into logically pieced stanzas,
determines a fundamental creativity,
in a writer's poetic style,
   which often
is subject to multiple interpretations,
as the reader parades the palisades of yearning
minds, anxious to critically dissect the literal
anatomy of words that typically characterize
the emboldened letters beyond.

The poems in this book represent multiple experiences rooted in everyday routine life abroad and in my native land, Cameroon.

Read and enjoy!

Part I: Learning and Responsibility: Finding the Inspiration to Excel

"Excellence is a fine motive for achievement,
if we stir our dreams in the right direction."

The Gift of Thanks

Thanks,
  For the gift of knowledge
that makes us intelligent;
  For the gift of wisdom,
that renders good judgment in the
mind of the wise;
  For the gift of humility,
that humbles one's self;
  For the gift of selflessness,
that simplifies our being;
  For the gift of honesty,
that enriches our spirit;
  For the gift of sharing,
that gives freely to others;
  And for the goodness of our hearts,
that exudes kindness in others in
  desperate moments of need.
In everything we say thank, you for in all these qualities
the rewards in heaven are tenfold.

(Memories of my Early and Later Years at Bowie State University)

"If the University does not teach a student to think, it has taught him nothing of genuine worth, has failed wide of its mark, and lastly, ... the University is not for a mindless mob but for the Talented Tenth"

....

"any student seriously committed to intellectual enterprise must begin, even in his under-graduate days, to create the embryo of a library of his own, for he needs not only standard text books but also books of extended reading; and what better guide can he have for this than his chosen field and allied disciplines and others farther afield in which he develops an interest of general culture, and where else should he find these books than in a university bookshop"
(Fonlon xii and xiv)

Freshman Class of Fall 2003
Knowledge

Wisdom, born of knowledge,
    A wise tool in the learning process.
So if patience and endurance
    breed knowledge,
then should not knowledge be the
    ultimate weapon for academic success?
Should it not be the breeding ground for
    future careerists rushing against the rising tide,
like stormy waves on the high seas?
    Therefore, hold your peace and be quiet,
until we combat the rising tide and calm
    the high seas in academic robes.

Then, shall we in all dignity and humility
    burst out in euphoria like gigantic balloons,
braving the strong winds,
    acknowledging knowledge that has defied
incompetence, mediocrity, and laziness by
    crossing the threshold to grasp that mere
piece of paper dangling in our hands, titled:
    First Degree!

Freshman Class of Spring 2004
The Beauty of My Soul

The beauty of my soul
lies in the way I carry myself.
Vanity and Pride trashed in the bin,
      while
humility and selflessness are paramount.

The beauty of my soul
lies in the way I relate to others.
A complaisant heart that easily blends
      with
the complacent nature of others.

The beauty of my soul
lies in my aspirations.
A vigorous zeal to pursue education
with a vengeance
      and
grab another honorable title.

Most importantly,
the beauty of my soul
lies in the way I relate to God,
living the first moment for the last,
and the last moment for the first,
      with
daily prayer, my watchword.

Only in such a way then will the richness
of my soul light up that ethereal
relationship between mankind
      and
the almighty one,
thereby splashing that ultimate reality
      in
our anxious faces.

The Pride of a Profession

Knowledge is something that you share
  and not something that you hide.

Knowledge is something that you exhibit
  and not something that you shelve.

Knowledge is something that you are proud of
  and not something that you are ashamed of.

Knowledge is something that you distribute
  and not something that you dump.

Knowledge is something that you invest in
  and not something that you squander.

Knowledge is something that you nurture
  and not something that you mishandle.

Knowledge is a golden gift to man
  so rather than treat it shabbily,
handle it with care,
  so it doesn't split into tiny pieces of glass
and be shattered forever.

That is why you should be proud of a skilled
profession like ours whose ultimate goal is the
  dissemination of ideas through multiple
channels of instruction.

FRESHMAN CLASS OF SPRING 2005
Academics

Is the vessel of hope which
floats like a leaf on a river
      and never sinks.

It maintains its purity of dryness
      and never wets.

If tampered with nonchalantly,
      it will sink,

Then stubbornly float again to
      challenge its aggressor,
thereby hiking the ladder to
      firmly stay on top.

But if it sinks and stubbornly
      refuses to float,

it will be buried with the
      muddy bottom
to become food for the fish
      losing its value forever.

      Who are you?
Would you float like a leaf in
a river and firmly stay on top?
Would you challenge your
aggressor if tampered with?
Or would you lose yourself in
the muddy bottom to become food
for the fish?

Challenges

Mirror my frustrations
on a typical class day;
Back and forth I rush.
My heavy bag strung
across my shoulder,
I rush building to building across campus,
breathless as I settle down.

Folders of assignments
piled on my table;
yet the weekend comes,
flying like a kite.
Two options I have:

Which should I choose?
Folders or leisure?

For the hectic weekend
just whisked past my ears
like the whispering winds,
as I am left to gamble ...
then ponder over my choices,
daring to negotiate challenges
that lie ahead, and
wrestle with a fate that
determines my future.

Are you ready for the task?
Let your conscience decide.

Bridges

Bridges are not built in a day,

----

ideas are not conceived in a day;

But challenge me to the task,

----

and I will defend the wisdom that

----

bridges me to a game of words,

----

beyond the conference room,

Starbucks, and the Paris salon.

Freshman Class of Fall 2005
Ambition

Is an intellectual weapon
that launches like a satellite,
skyrockets my dreams,
and mingles it with the stars

As fragile as a wounded heart,
it staggers and stumbles, then
adjusts to life's chronic ways,
diseased by rampant irrationalities
in making decisive decisions

Tainted by incessant temptations;
springboards of intellectual disruptions
which fling me in a dungeon of floating
meditations,
I cling on to the stars.

So will I hold on to the barriers
of my dangling fate
by ambitiously launching like Discovery,
my future career goals
in a universe where starry dreams
are attainable.

Are you like the crew ready to launch?
Because if you aren't, then you are in the
wrong place.
But if you are, then space-walk with me.

Freshman Class of Fall 2006
Adjustments

The dawn of a new stage
    in life;
is a major symbol
    of
boat-bridge—

transitions in life,
adaptation to new environment,
higher expectations,
respect for others,
wisdom in the mind,
growth in age,
maturity in character,
consciousness of time,
focus on studies,
commitment to goals,
    and
effectiveness in achieving them
    through
meeting deadlines,
braving challenges,
and rejecting flimsy excuses.

Such is the flexible synopsis
of adjustment that must be
tagged in your brains.

Freshman Class of Spring 2006
Academic Obsession

The bookworms of academia
rise up early in the morning
with an agenda,
ready for execution.

They scurry around
dorm rooms, hallways,
classrooms, cafeterias,
and bookshelves,
hunting for knowledge
buried in a thick alphabet of
encyclopedic pages.

Quick pen in hand,
notepads on tables,
they leaf through pages,
     skim,
     scan,
and speedily jot down
important material obtained
from libraries,
to complete
research or term papers.

They embrace websites and the Internet
with an impatient obsession to devour,
then consume useful information
that serves as the determining formula
for success,
inherently pursuing attainable goals,
in a harsh world of reality that offers
tempting alternatives.

Thus,
will I also become a bookworm of
academia, vigorously anxious to commit
myself not only to libraries but also to
a modern technology, which I can use
as a weapon for my academic advancement
and success?

Class of Summer 2006
Summertime

Summer is a time for white sandy beaches
and bikini swimsuits.
It is a time for partying and dancing.
It is also a time for trips and vacations.

But this summertime is different for me.

My summer '06 is a time
for academic achievement.
It is a time for knowledge acquisition
using skilled techniques, labeled in
multiple rhetorical modes of
writing essays that uniquely
      model,
      define,
      clarify,
      upgrade,
and
      develop
standardized novice skills, previously
presupposed as consumable A-rate.

Here I come then,
scuba diving into my summer English course
with the sole purpose of netting an A, then
striding it to the next level in the fall,
with a load of optimism.

So hard work, focus, consistency, and feedback,
honk me in the speeding diesel as a novice
passenger who rumbles through the tedious
phases to reach a final destination.

Freshman Class of Spring 2007
Predictions

Like a soldier battling anonymous insurgents
on the battlefield
are an ultimate means to combat doubtful uncertainties
that cloud the mind at the beginning of a new semester.

The courage to brave the challenge and defeat the enemy
arm to arm and weapon to weapon
is synonymous to combating doubtful uncertainties
with a power of positive thinking,
that resurges innate, subconscious talents over duly suppressed
through multiple years of doubtful uncertainty about the
strength of my intelligence.

Therefore, as I rush through this semester, with
pen and laptop in hand,
my writing skills will ignite and sprout like the seasonal
cherry blossoms whose multiple colors depict its
attractiveness as mine will be manifested through the
multiplicity of my alternating writing modes, revised and
structured on paper, rather than on a cherry tree.

My predictions will border on my long-term goals as a college
student, ready to enter the next phase of an intense, critically
assessed writing competition that will exit me with a pass
grade, that has boldly overcome uncertainties,
through the power of forceful,
                    thinking …
determination …
                                    and
        success,
true only to the dreams of Martin Luther King.

Freshman Class of Fall 2007
Bridging the Golden Gate

On the call of my name,
　　as I tailored my way
through the majestic crowd
　　of scholarly graduates
to receive my meritorious diploma
　　on the prestigious platform
of my ceremonious award,
　　before my mentors, parents, and invited guests,
tears of joy filled my eyes
　　and flooded down my cheeks,
for I had just exited the threshold of
　　one golden gate,
and bridged into another systematic
　　transatlantic parade
that manicured its way
　　into the universe of my future
career dreams and goals.

　　Now,
after having traversed one pinnacle of
　　life's hasty perennial journey,
I therefore advanced to the intellectual
　　premise of a college campus
wherein
　　I paraded myself among the ranks of future
Wall Street magnates,
career journalists,
famous lawyers and doctors,
congressmen and women,
to name but a few,
　　assembled on the campus of my university
like budding seeds on the farm fields
　　on this first day of class.

So, as I muscle up and energize to tackle the
    immense workload that validates the goals
of my academic advancement and stay here
    this semester, I am soundly determined that in
the next four years,
    I will be robed, ranked, and filed once more among
the multitude of graduates who climb the stage
    on the call of their name,
to elegantly exit the podium that bridges them
    into another golden gate of intellectual dreams.

Class of Fall 2005
The Reader

Obsessed with words
paraded in lines,
stumps his brains
    with volumes of knowledgeable
    material,
as military brigades stomp their feet,
for a Fourth of July parade.

The Power of Words

Crafted in letters, is so exciting
for the mind to absorb.
Like a waterfall, it flows and
penetrates its depth,
leaving us stunned, perplexed, and
aware of an active subconscious mind
that only awakes when consciously
explored by a conscious conscience
that games our thoughts.

It builds momentum over the years,
matures and hardens like brick walls,
only to explode molten lava on
mountaintops, valleys, and hills,
spilled in offensive themes of diction,
dramatized through
      bribery,
corruption,
      favoritism,
anarchy, and fear;
that mold in the beer parlors,
and offices of manipulative
civil servants, trapped in a
reckless web of …
unaccountability!

It navigates its spill across the
Atlantic Ocean,
scampers to the desktops
and conference rooms
of intellectual panels,
who proudly like peacocks
dissect the anatomy of acts and scenes
into comic strips of traditional dance,
forum, and theater.

So has the power of words,
scripted in satire,
spilled comic rhetoric,
dramatized in the art of theater,
so then,
depicting the hassles that
engulf
a modern society like ours,
humorously leaving us …

gasping for more!

<u>Freshman Class of Fall 2008</u>
My Triple Combination

A Reader Reads with a Critical Mind
A Writer Writes with an Articulate
Stapling of Diction that Intensely
Captivates, then Reverberates
in the Mind of the Reader,
and you, the Student,
Absorbs with an Absolute
Idiosyncratic Pattern, Reflective of your Personality.

Food for thought:
What idiosyncratic pattern defines your own personality?

Freshman Class of Spring 2008
My Gut Instinct

My challenges of today
      are _____
my rewards of tomorrow.
My rewards of tomorrow
      are _____
my profits of the future.

While patience is scaled on a pedestal of trials
and struggles,
Success is reaped from the priceless fruits that
      I sow

As _____
my friendship nurtures, then matures into fruition;
my career is built, then pursued into old age;
Lives are changed by the career paths that I pursue,
      but _____
The challenges that bridge me to a bright future,
are the *gold mines* that I harvest, then harness,
since _____
my successes of today,
      are _____
built on a melodious cord of hope,
resurrected from the lost and weary voices of
past ancestral generations,
bonded by a lost hope that obscures current reality
so long as I cling on to chance,
      as _____
a response to my *gut instinct*.

Class of Summer 2008
Memories of My Summer

Four years from now,
on the verge of grabbing my BA,
memories of my summer will linger
in my mind like clean white linen
pegged on a dry line.

Memories of an exciting transition from high school to
college will quickly fade like an exciting dream, turned
unexpectedly and tediously, stressful like a man swept
through a tornado blast.

Self-confidence in my ability to read and write confidently,
as amplified and exaggerated by my previously mediocre
talented skills will quickly plummet and be swallowed
by a thunderous windstorm that will sweep me through
the tide of a revolting, agony-ridden state of self-induced
motivation, to grab the bulk of assignments due on dates
principled only by my inert motive to succeed and not be
terrified by the increasing demands of college professors.

So,
will I exude confidence, hold myself in high esteem,
mature in my attitude, and pursue nothing this summer
but the sole goal to succeed and achieve a satisfactory level
in my current quest for undergraduate reading and
writing in this first year of college?

Such is my intent of rewarding my high school teachers for
having motivated me to pursue a great path toward an achievement
that has routed me into the arms of campus independence,
and liberated me from the claws of parental control
which loudly parrots the screams in my mind that:

"I am now on my own! What does freedom and
time management mean to me?"

Then memories of four years past will quickly speed through
my mind to paste a tasty smile of victory on my face,
when I hold the degree solidly in my hand, thereby,
authenticating my success and enduring path to achievement.

Freshman Class of Fall 2009
Gambling with Opportunities

If in the journey of life, the greatest things that we can do
to the best of our human knowledge and ability cannot be
done when we must do it, then we fail as individuals to comply
to the fundamental rules that inspire and govern our daily lives.

If we cannot make good use of opportunities that knock
on our doors at opportune moments in history, then we
delay, to our own detriment, fortune's goals that gear us
toward a productive future;

and,
if we are passive dreamers over the things that beckon us
to succeed in crucial moments, when time is of the essence,
then we lack the stamina to confront challenges by manifesting
ignorance of knowledge that has eluded us in our bygone days
of fragile dependence.

But if we awaken to embrace and explore our needs, with a
passion to succeed,

if we brave challenges without complaint, then we leave the
doors wide open,
since when gambling with opportunities, there must always
be a winner and a loser obsessed with the roller-coaster roulette,
as it spins its way toward fortune or perhaps misfortune's goals.

So climb the bus and ride on if you must,
or climb not, if you lack faith in yourself.

From the desk of
Professor Langmia,

Good luck, study hard, and have a successful semester!

Red Marks on Their Papers

A rush of wind suddenly whisks past my ear
as I marathon to the mountaintop,
so breathless, yet longing for a pause
on this unending trip of incessant
paperwork, with red pen in hand.

Lost in thought, I start sliding from the top,
with no regard for grammatical improprieties,
juxtaposed in strings of fragmented phrases,
woven together like coffee baskets.

Succumbing to defeat, I yield not to pity but to the
developmental skills that will ripen the
fruit of my lectured labor, long before I percolate
my inner senses to explore necessary
material for fresh beginners, though the red marks
on these papers before my eyes stretch like an
elastic band strapped to their folded form.

Class of Fall 2010
Fragmented Syntax

The paradox of words synchronized in fragmented syntax
juxtaposes the connotation of meaning that streams through
the mind of a reader.

What audience are you then addressing? As if one were to probe
into your mindset, and strive to dissect parables construed in
singular thoughts, unknown to the audience like some ancient
Greek rhetorician's model of fragments.

So deconstruct the puzzle and render my lips worthy of decoding
meaning in sentence patterns that are syllabically antithetical, lest
I should be drowned in a pool of words that lack the disciplinary
rules of standard, constructive English, be you poet or other.

Class of Spring 2010
Shed off the Cloak

Shed off the cloak and leave it behind,
before you cross this premise of intellectual myth,
for it is old, worn, tattered, and it has outlived its usefulness.

Its function has moved a step closer to grip an innate
personality that usually clings to someone for support, as
if it was a total dependent, with no voice to claim as its own.

So, isn't it a shame that you cling so tight and lose your
independent foothold when it is time for you to make
profitable decisions toward a destined future?

So I say, let go and blend in with the crowd of future
triumphant elites who will weather the storm for the
next generation.

Ring the bell, shed off the cloak, and make the next decisive move
for a better future since tomorrow recognizes no victims in
hallways overwhelmed with the burden of coursework,
for that is the stark reality of campus life which supersedes
all the other distractions that come with a college education.

From the desk of Professor Langmia,
Have a great semester!

Part II: Religious: A Vision of Light

" In his hand he held a small scroll that had been opened.
He placed his right foot on the sea and his left foot on the land,
and he cried out in a loud voice as the lion roars." (Revelation 10:
2-3)

In loving memory of Dad
Live the Experience

When death penetrated your soul,
and pierced your heart,
in that _____
unexpected moment
of blissful happiness,
when life's hassles overwhelmed your spirit
and buzzed past your eardrums,
you tended to float in a whirlwind of dreams
as memories of loved ones faded,
in a vision of an afterlife that
bombarded your brains,
as with a grim smile on your lips,
and rosary in hand,
you did lie in death,
as opposed to the amusing smile
that you had on your lips in life.

Such was the moment when you started living the
Experience _____!

Did you live that experience, Daddy?

Last Moments

Oh, that the wild, whispering wind
will blow away this feeling
of loss, insecurity, and madness.
Oh, that it will defy this reality,
visible in my eyes,
a cruel, painful, nightmarish vision of
death's cold grip on a desperate soul,
clinging on to life on this late December
midnight of Wednesday the 13th.

As I lie on my bed, alone at this hour,
dreaming of a long trip in a white Toyota
with Father, daughter, and family,
cruising in the dim light of a weary journey,
 echoed in syllabic dirges,
I anxiously search for him, with a grim smile
on my patched lips.

Yet, I see him not, for his seat is empty,
as my hand sinks onto leather, as pitch dark
as the night itself.

So suddenly then, I hear a voice calling,
in the wee hours of the morning,
and I wake up still with that grim smile
on my lips, still searching as I rush to the
window, fling it wide open to the sound of the voice,
still calling my name.

The door, I open, and they rush in,
but to wear my shoes and go I must, then
in sleepwalked madness, I rush and stumble up
the stairs and fall face down, battered and
shattered like a worn tire.

But go, I must, too.

I am like a withered leaf that has just
fallen off an autumn tree _____
I am slowly going down! down! down! and under,
as I see a dark bottomless pit. Somebody help me!
lest I should drown in my sorrow and be gone.
Gone? To where? Isn't that what just happened to Dad?

Reality sets in like a shockwave.
A life lived so soon, yet gone so abruptly … soon.
When did sixty-five years swing by so fast?
Isn't human existence a mere shadow of death?
Yet the cold, smeary hands of death echoes
this grim reminder:

I am death, king of the world.
Keep the torchlight burning
and watch out for me, so when I come,
with my iron fist I will gather the flock
branded by the light to greener pastures
reserved for thee.

So cling on to that crystal image reminiscent of
your last vision, lest be it that snatches your soul in
those last desperate moments as you cling on to life
with a word of prayer on your pale purple lips,
for when the spirit comes to seek your repentant soul,
it will lavish your silent lips with an incredible smile that will
serve as a memorabilia for future generations to come.

A Dad's Legacy

Before you passed away, you built a mansion
that was planted like a solid rock in the intellectual
minds and lives of those that you transformed.

Not the kind that was standing on marble and gold,
tall, and skyrocketing like a satellite in the sky,
but one that was rooted in the educated minds that
you bred and was nowhere to harvest.

But if you were there now to look back at the fruits of your
labor, and endeavor, I say, you would be proud of the ones
whose lives you touched.

So, as your spirit transmigrates into others, and lives on,
may your ways be emulated by those you left behind,
so their spiritual lives may be touched, since your rewards
in heaven will be plentiful, and bountiful.

Sunrise at My Window

As I lie on my bed,
staring outside on
this early Friday morning,
blinding rays of sunlight forcefully
burst through green tree leaves, to deeply
penetrate the beautiful white curtains of my
wide apartment window at Briarwood.

A stream of thoughts invade my mind
as I ponder over the greatness of the almighty one
who has created such sunshine that boldly penetrates
my bedroom window.

With the sign of the cross, I fervently begin to pray.
I thank God
for his goodness to me;
for the sunshine that penetrates my window;
for the mighty oak trees that overlook my window;
for my two kids, Brandon and Gabriel, anxious to
type on the computer as they keep hitting the keyboard;
for the food that we eat and the clothes that we wear.

Then,
I think of my dad long gone from the beauty of such
natural scenery, as in my mind's eye, I visualize
Daddy in his resting place smiling and laughing and I say,
Daddy was a talented writer,
Daddy was a conversationalist,
Daddy was a free thinker,
Daddy was a linguist,
Daddy was a loving father of eight,
Daddy adored the Virgin Mary.

Reason why in his last moment of pain,
surrendering his last breath,

he had this telltale smile on his lips,
with imaginary visions of Maria
beckoning him to follow a path of light
that transcended the universe of a previous life
gone in a second of blissful happiness.

Such is the tale of your last breath,
faded into the memory of your loved ones,
yet inspired by your gift of fatherly tenderness
and love, as alive as the burning flame that has
immortalized your living years,
        and
enkindled in our hearts forever the early sunlight
that now penetrates my bedroom window.

The Rustling Tide

Way above my tiny little frame,
My eyes are quickly drawn, then trapped in a comic
episode of Mother Nature's revolving rustling tide
that exhibits gray clouds rushing loudly and anxiously
against the blue, up in the livid skies,
as the windy whispering leaves hurl, then battle furiously
with shredded tree branches,
tantamount to a "the Rock" wrestling match of champions
that needs a desperate winner on this shy, sunny,
yet bitter cold, wintry New Year's Eve morning of
December 31.

I am still basking in the joyous feel of Christ's
birth, with rejuvenated feelings of love and
a rare gut feeling that consumes my spirit.

With visions of Christ lying in a manger;
then graced with the presence of three wise men
from the east who come with myrrh, frankincense,
and gold to honor and worship him,
the anxieties of joy that usually bring tears to my
eyes during this New Year's hype has not changed one bit.

Yet, only the location and status of my being has changed
over the years.

Blended with the drama of Christmas celebrations this year is
the excited warmth of winter graduations at Bowie State,
a symbolic reminder of president-elect Barack Obama's
historic visit to this campus.

But vicissitudes of hope, generated by his historic victory as the forty-fourth president of the United States, build momentum, as the drumbeats of change sweep across America in the midst of struggle.

Yet hope though forsaken by the people is revived in dreams and aspirations that depend on financial stability.

So the rustling tide, caught in the euphoric drama of
the moment, will it stabilize in the next year or continue
into the next four?

Only time will tell.

Rhapsodies in the Wind

Two friends once met
in the four walls of a university classroom
in the late sixties of a historical period,
richly endowed with a deep-rooted
    Anglophone culture of
    ancestral worship
    and traditional deities,
recently juxtaposed with a colonial
    conversion of
    innocent,
    ignorant minds,
trapped in a mirage of faith.

They sat on the same desks
    were taught by the same professors
    of great minds, wisdom, and talent
    in the likes of
Bernard Nsokika Fonlon.

And so began a raving ambition
nurtured in their minds to
mountain their talent in volumes of
panhandles,
newly discovered.

Ambition lent them a hand
in the pursuit of different scholarships
as they excelled in their degree programs
and so be it that they parted ways.

One went to Leeds in England

The other went to Southern Illinois University in Carbondale, USA

The former was initialed

K. W. J.
Author of the thrilling *White Man of God*
The latter was initialed
J. A. N.
Author of the famous *Taboo Love*

So, the chiming bells have tolled at last
and six feet under now,
their memorabilia remain but
corded melodies,
rhapsodized
on the debating tables of literate minds,
lipped together by conferences, and
book-signing events.

And so in death, they lie not in death
but in a musical drumbeat of timelessness,
that echoes their
passions;
                              dreams;
             and
achievements;
published in paperback and hardcover
for readers to read and explore the
world's diversity in an era of
postcolonial modernism.

In Memory of My Venezuelan Colleague

As my colleagues and I sit on the pews of
St. John's, on this cold and windy February
morning of spring 2005, with white snow
caked to the ground,
  I think of a friend,
            a brother,
            a colleague,
and I start to weep.

I think of a time,
when he hummed songs aloud in his
native Venezuelan tongue, as he
majestically strolled to the copy room
opposite my office with a set of papers in hand.
Then I would laugh aloud, and shout to him,
"Hi, Professor Vidal!"
And he would turn his head, smile at me, then
reply heartily,
"Hi, Professor Langmia!"
in that deep, musical baritone, splashed with
a Spanish accent,
shortly before getting into the copy room.

Then we would chat, and converse amusingly,
while he photocopied, and I graded papers.
I would tell him how I used to dance pechanga,
merengue, and salsa, in Monte Christo, in my
native Cameroon.
Oh! how he used to lift his head, and burst into
loud laughter!

It was always such a pleasure to share cultural
experiences, each time he went back and forth
to the copy room.

So, as I sit at St John's at this moment and weep,
as my colleagues weep too, and watch the coffin of a
colleague placed at the altar,
as I listen to the priest preach about the passage of time,
as I watch Professor V's look-alike brother and his
family grieve with ashy faces,
as I listen to Dr. Brenda Do-Harris recite Alfred Lord Tennyson's
"Crossing the Bar,"
as I join the funeral cortege with Denise, Shansa, and Kimberly,
as the wind blows on our faces, unprotected from the cold
at the cemetery,
and as he is lowered six feet under, into his grave,
I walk back to the car with my head bowed, lost in thought.

I feel like a loner who has lost touch with the reality of life,
as I ponder;

Where will my colleague's soul, which has now separated from
his body, go to?
Where will my soul go to after it separates from my body?

I think hard, and hard, and hard, and hard!

I exit the cemetery with Tennyson's elegiac piece of farewell
to Professor V. as I recite:
    "And may there be no sadness of farewell,
      When I embark;"
    For,
    "The flood may bear me far,
    I hope to see my pilot face to face
    When I have crossed the bar."

Good-bye, Prof. V., as you "cross the bar," to depart no more.

Illusions

Mirrored in my mind's eye
an oval glass box,
spinning in midair
and,
in the center of the spin,
an immaculate, spotless white vision
of the Virgin Mary,
garbed in an ox-blood robe
belted at the waist like a priest's cassock.

With a crown of charming red roses,
mingled with starry, enigmatic flashlights
adorning her veil,
she in all humility bows her head,
while leaning her chin on the tips of
fingers, entangled in a blue rosary
weeping tears, that form puddles of rainbow
colors dripping to her feet.

Then,
as she raises that heavenly vision of delight,
drenched with tender tears of gloom for a
lost generation that has vastly rejected her
son's message of salvation, while embracing
violence,
she weeps and prays for this generation
that has partially distorted biblical interpretations by
brainwashing innocent souls to a hellish furnace of perpetual,
suicidal bondage like slaves chained on a ship deck, ready for
the master's hundredfold lashes of bloody death.

As the glass box whirls faster and faster in the air,
my heartbeat accelerates faster too as I
struggle to come to grips with this sudden reality
unfolding before my eyes so rapidly.

I struggle in vain to focus on this
dreamy apparition that has invaded my vision,
spinning upward toward the great heavens
like her son, Jesus, when he ascended and
vanished like a thin cloud in the midst of
his apostles.

Behold, rainbow colors as fiery as fireworks explode
in the sky and heavenly images cloud my memory!

I wake up instantly, drenched in my own sweat.
Breathing heavily, visions of her retreating in the glass box
against the mysterious clouds slowly vanish before my eyes as I
awake to the reality of my current life, huddled against the
headboard of my bed.

Was I dreaming?

Scrolls

Was I transcending into another world?
Or
was I still on planet Earth?

The message was designed on papyrus;
scribbled in Roman bold letters, like
in the biblical days of Moses on the
peak of Mount Sinai, receiving the ten
commandments from Yahweh.

Against a moonless, starless,
pitch-dark night sky,
I could see unfolding, lengthy scrolls engulfed
by symbolic rays of flames that lighted, then
paraded the night sky in a pantomime of choreographed
dance.

A mighty, mysterious finger touched the words and read
the messages aloud, while the scrolls lapped and danced
against each other.

Behold,
I could neither read nor understand
the messages that were written on the scrolls
because of its ancient Roman bold letters.

Trapped in the midst of scrolls,
my anxiety soared, then burst into
wild flames of anticipation for the unknown!
What was the message hidden behind the flamed scrolls?
In vain, I struggled to understand.

Then a vision of angels with angelic voices
suddenly burst forth before my eyes and started
singing, in Latin, songs that I could not comprehend.

High spirited, yet very confused,
I started trembling as a sudden fear gripped my
rocky spirit, and I fell on my face flat down, thinking.
What message did Yahweh have for me?
Why could I not read the message on the scrolls?
Was my soul unworthy of the Lord at this time?

I know not!
Only the almighty one has the answers,
for when I raised my head,
and looked up at the dark night sky,
everything had pallidly vanished before
my own very eyes.

The Rising Tide of Judgment Day

On the rising tide of judgment day,
we will arise tall and high, as
scattered across the tombs of the dead,
in the city of Jerusalem and beyond, will
be the souls of the risen, as
we will all, dead or alive, rise to meet our maker.

For he will come in glory and pageantry,
Lo! amidst the loudness of the trumpets
and the horns, the dove will descend from
the skies, flanked by golden angels, riding
high on the wings of the king.

He will spread his wings wide, and the angels and
saints in heaven will sound the trumpets of joy,
doomed to end this passage of time that has marked
and scarred a generation of lost souls, prone to sin
and evil; so scornful of godliness, yet aware of his
invincible presence always hovering in our midst.

Then we will smile and raise our voices, if one, we
have still, to say, "Hola! ye sons and daughters of Adam
and Eve! Where forth go ye, for we will follow thee to
the ends of the earth?"

Eastertide

The celebration of a resurrection;
the passion of the world's greatest
celebrity,
born to a carpenter and a maiden girl
turned spiritual housewife.
The lone salvation of a humble man
who once walked the streets centuries ago,
garbed in robes and sandals that gathered the dust
from whose image sprung man as he
celebrated the living word with converted
companions, turned apostles.

So has the death of a king,
borne new life in a sinful world
through the generous compassion of the holy one;
as,
salvation born of the resurrection then has
liberated man's sinful spirit from eternal
damnation.
So shall true believers in the afterlife
sail through the golden gate, saved by
a resurrection celebrated at Eastertide.

The Funeral Cortege

Drove by me one Wednesday at midday,
   on the stretch of Laurel-Bowie, as I rushed home from
a busy intense morning of workshops on Bowie State campus.

   Then the remarkable yellow stickers on the
windshield made me ponder, then contemplate
   the fate of he who therein lay,
for on that day I knew him not, but saw him I did, in
   his last moment of transcendence from the mortal, to
the spiritual, as his hearse cruised by.

But to this day, memories of the funeral cortege
   that drove past me one Wednesday at midday,
as I rushed home from work, have not eluded my mind.

So to this soul I pray you rest and share in the meal of the
   reposed, as your days of struggle are long gone and over,
and only your spirit still dwells in the hearts of your loved ones,
   on this night of intense blizzard with mountains of snow
piled high on the ground like the pyramids of Giza, as I think about
   your life, which I knew not, but saw only as a passerby at a
glance.

   So further, I pray that your soul may rest in peace, and yield the
fruit of your labor in the afterlife, which you now share with the
   others.

Where to Look for Me

Do not look for me in marble halls and golden palaces
where kings and queens squander and plunder,
then fornicate and cavort shamelessly.

Do not look for me in hidden mortuaries and golden
tombs when I am worn, torn, and gone.

Do not look for me in golden city malls and Broadway halls
where vanity lurks, where spendthrift celebrities are
trapped in a mirage of shadows, overdosed by an
irate paparazzi that lasts only for a moment in time,
splashed on the tabloids of magazine covers.

Look for me on street corners and in dark alleys, wrapped
in the blanket of the oppressed, homeless, and forgotten.

Look for me in the unmarked graves of heroic soldiers who lost
their lives in the battlefields of glory, defending their nation
from ruthless psychopaths riddled with apathetic religious
    fantasies.

Look for me in the graveyard of the downtrodden and belated
    citizen
who died materially poor but spiritually wealthy, for there I lay my
head on the shoulder of the cemetery guard, keeping watch as the
clock chimes *tick, tock.*

Look for me where the meek and the lowly dwell for in their
distant eyes, I lurk in the shadow of darkness, consuming
their lowly spirits and strengthening their passionate souls.

Look for me before Sunday morning mass on the steps of the
    cathedral
where lepers beg, and dine, and stampede for coins from
the familiar parishioner, whose footsteps cling and clang to

the beat of the tambourine, echoing loudly from
the church walls.

Look for me before the cock crows every morning, because
there I wait anxiously to pacify the next soul who yearns
for my father's abode.

Look for me where the downtrodden dwell and lay their weary
heads on worn mats to doze, and daze in emptiness and oblivion.

Look for me where the graffiti walls and homeless shelters
embrace and kiss so that tomorrow, you will have a story to tell
and that story will spread beyond the banks of raging oceans,
whispering winds, and tumultuous thunderstorms, so by the time
that I return, you will be able to look for me easily and find me
    right
where I belong, in my father's abode.

Then listen to the voice, and the call, and the fall of great
empires and nations, for on that last day, I will know no
hue nor hair that did not of my father's cup drink.
But rather, I will behold, embrace, and beckon to those that of
my father's cup drank, to sit on the dining table of kings and
    queens,
and partake of the ethereal feast that will be celebrated in my
    father's
kingdom; a feast that will last forever and see no end, since the last
    day
of judgment would have so passed away, and the old would have
given way to the new.

Life's Hassles

In Memory of Father Patrick Adesso

Where there is life, there is death
    Where there is death, there is life.

What, therefore, is life without death
    if there is no death without life
in the lifelong servitude,
    and hassle of a selfless servant
of our lord and master Jesus Christ,
    lost in a mysterious quagmire of man's
tragic obsession with brutal death?

    Celebrate therefore his servitude in his lifetime
of service to mankind in praise of Yahweh.
    For those whose spirits he touched, and
those whose troubles he resolved in his
    lifetime, he did so with joy and humility.
So too will his rewards in heaven multiply,

for the life he lived in service to God and mankind.

Tribulations of True Love

True love is extraordinary.
It is neither wasteful nor boastful,
but useful, and tender.

It is neither arrogant nor defiant,
but gentle, and polite.

It is neither exploitative nor deceitful,
but truthful, and honest.

It is neither corrupt nor manipulative,
but transparent, and clean.

It is neither hypocritical nor tearful,
but sincere, humble, and happy.

It is neither primitive nor evil,
but imbibes civilized attitudes bred of proper
moral etiquettes that exude self-confidence
in society, lest it should hide behind a cloud of dust
and bond with the enemy in times of danger.

It is neither disrespectful nor presumptuous,
but respectful, and unassuming.

It is neither possessive nor judgmental of others
based on hearsay,
but confronts reality face to face.

It does not pride itself boastfully of someone's failures,
but commends success with reward.

True love, in the end,
is neither chaotic nor dramatic,

but calm, and self-assuring.

True love, behold, singles out the enemy and chases
it down the lane, so the angels that surround its head
would not depart in fury and abandon,
lest the unsteady mind should pedal its way into the
boots of the unseen soldier, battling the demons of its past.

Dances at the Church

I remember the day in my childhood
when with Jacinta, Vivian, and Cecilia,
we laughed and danced in circles behind
pews at the spacious entrance within the church
at St. Peter's on Saturday afternoons.

Then, the skirts of our tired dresses would fly over
our laps as we would ignorantly lift them up and
cover our heads while jamming into each other
like a pack of wolves.

For we knew nothing then, and nothing knew us,
but God above, who saw our ignorance, read our
innocent minds, and cuddled us to his heart.

But if I knew then what I know now,
I would have been horrified at the lack of respect
in the temple of the Lord to lift a dress and dance
around crazily while exposing nudity.

So forgive us, dear Lord, for childhood is nothing like
adulthood, where knowledge and experience beats
imagination, and disciplines its whereabouts, so
misconceived misbehaviors will not be construed as
sinful but the lack of a good sense of judgment,
due to ignorance at childhood.

From the Heart of an Anxious Woman

I was no stranger in that year to the painful anxiety
that usually gripped the heart of an anxious
African woman newly wed.

I had anticipated with every nerve of excitement
the luscious feel that usually came with the
aftermath of a settlement in life to conception,
having never categorized myself under the list of
presupposed, prejudged barrenness that critics
hyped on the likes of us in the city of
my native land.

So I anticipated in all honesty that procreation would
dangle its feet at me in any given moment before
society laughed at me in the face, in the back,
and in hidden corners, branding me as a woman of
barrenness, since the likes of us were treated
no better than outcasts.

But behold, that moment of anxiety turned
      into weeks,
      into months,
      into years,
as I then labeled myself under the list of the branded,
for my society would not control its critical weapon
of ridicule on my persona.

Yet, I held on to a thin thread of hope,
that grimly turned into a wild imagination
of despair that usurped my thoughts and tortured
my inner spirit day and night, as obsession fiercely
gripped my mind with an urgency to have a baby.

Then in the midst of this confusion and anxiety,
I suddenly had an unusual dream one night, with
images of a chubby baby boy raised high above the air,
as I strained in wonder and amazement to see this
phantom of my imaginary dreams sprout to life
before my bewildered eyes.

As I started straining to catch the baby, I heard an inner voice say:

"Why worry, young woman?
Rest your anxiety and trust in God, for He will deliver."

Yet as I flashback eight years later and contemplate
the strength of my faith,
I cannot but wonder and thus be gratefully stupefied,
for isn't my son a late-night manifestation of God's
apparition that visited me at a low moment of despair
to curb imminent anxieties generated by society's
critical eye?

Such is the fate of the childless woman in my society,
most often labeled with the stigma of barrenness and ridicule,
when children become a rare commodity in the marriage.

Lack of Foresight

On my way home from the Shell gas station on an
Easter after mass morning of Sunday, April 17th,
a terrible lack of judgment and foresight made me
take the wrong left turn at the streetlight on
197/Laurel Bowie,
so suddenly, I almost collided with a pale
red truck heading full speed in my direction.

Then I heard the loud hoot and stopped so abruptly,
with my heart thumping in my mouth in total
confusion.

A second I had, to make the decision of a lifetime,
with my two sons huddled in the backseats.
In a flash, I sped on, into the extreme left lane, and
exited the junction.

Then it struck me so seriously how death usually
preyed on our lives at unexpected moments of
indecision.

For when I left the house early that Easter morning,
the question was:
had I thought about death at all which was on this day,
a symbolic celebration of Christ's own resurrection?

My Heritage

We once were a stereotyped people
living in a typical traditional setup
in a stretch of land that projected
a customized lifestyle of traditional
      ethics and beauty;
in cowries,
              camwood,
ngwashis,
      wrappers,
and jujus,
plus a traditional worship of gods
depicting
the sun, the moon,
the stars, the trees,
the harvest, and all that be.

The village seers predicted our future,
determined our lifestyle,
poured libations on the doorsteps of
our compounds,
predicted the oracles in caves and shrines,
and determined our fate.

Then the white man came, with a Bible in hand
and so began the web of deceit, destruction, and
exploitation.
They destroyed our oracle,
and labeled it pagan.
They destroyed our jujus,
and labeled it evil.
They destroyed our ancestral worship
of trees, moon, and stars,
and labeled it satanic.
They destroyed everything,
and introduced us to God.

But as I ponder now over our fate,
I also contemplate and wonder
if we ever understood what was
in the Bible and also,
if we ever understood what was going on,
nor the revolutionary twist that would impact
a stereotyped culture that had been viciously
uprooted from its base,
fatally synonymous to Okwonkwo's tragedy.

Sunset in the Blues

There is a lone tree in the fields
basking in the star-studded image
of a retreating dusky sunshine,
of striking blues and yellowish gray.

Sunset, be my guest, lest my eyes
should drown in your mirage of colors.

Against the green fields in the plains
is a mysterious rainbow,
set against a gray sky that slowly
dims into sunset.

The fluffy clouds, all white and blue,
bask in the beauty of its labor
all transitioned to sunrise
at the dawn of day.

The Insane Beggar

Thaddeus and I were seated
across from each other on a crate
in front of Carrefour Elig-Essono's
Miramar bar, one busy Friday afternoon
after school.

Holding a bottle of 33" Export,
and a few hundred CFA coins in hand,
and none in mine,
he cozily relaxed, chatted with
colleagues, and sipped from his
beer bottle, while I in turn,
sipped my Fanta soda.

Abruptly, I saw him running across the street,
dodging oncoming cars.
He looked so haggard, dirty, bearded, and stinky.
Sweating profusely in his dirty white "aguada,"
and screaming all to himself,
I could tell upon close observation of his hollow eyes
that this was a madman, prowling the streets
of downtown Yaoundé at midday, wrought in abject
hunger, starvation, fury, and restlessness.
He hadn't eaten a good meal for days,
nor had a good night's rest.
Nobody had shown him love nor given him love. Frightened, I
    watched him run
straight to Thaddeus, stretch his right
arm out, and loudly command desperately
and aggressively,
"Give me money. I am hungry!"

Looking him straight in the eye,

Thaddeus refused to surrender his CFA coins.
The madman insisted.
But my colleague roughly shoved him off with the coined palm,
    complaining that he should go look for a job:
Va chercher le travaille!

I urged Thaddeus to give him the coins,
but he adamantly refused!
Quickly,
I sent my hand into my backpack,
grabbed some coins and was about to give
the beggar when he instantly cursed,
turned around, and fled across the street abruptly,
blowing the dust with his dirty yellow flip-flops.

Strangely,
the beggar never asked me for money
yet, I was sitting right across from Thaddeus

Why?

Could it be that Jesus had come to Thaddeus in
rags but was offhandedly rejected?

Summer vacation came and went!

On my return to school, I learnt
that Thaddeus had died abruptly of a sudden illness.
I was stunned.

Yet to this day,
I often contemplate and wonder:
could it be that
Christ visited Thaddeus in rags?
Why did the madman not ask me for money?

Brothers and sisters in Christ,
be sure not to miss Jesus when he
comes to you,
for
He will come in rags and not in riches.

Lunatic at Dawn

Instead of a cock's crow, the heart-wrenching cry
of a solitary lunatic would wake me up in the
wee hours of dawn.
Startled, I would wake up, scared to death, with my
heart pounding in my ears.

Then it would dawn on me—Oh! It is him again!
Would he never go away?
A homeless lunatic in a shelter-less shelter under a
baobab tree, situated on a main crossroad in the
heart of the city!

A busy street that accommodates foreign embassies
and a town hall, where prostitutes lurk in the heart
of midnight.

All of these clustered together to breed an eerie air of
upper-class nuance that shields the plight of depraved
paupers turned lunatics, sleeping and walking the streets
in search of lost aspirations, unfulfilled dreams, and a
bite to eat.

So it is that a lone lunatic with a voice to sing blended his
weary songs with that of the birds in the darkness of dawn
in this solitary location with none but the sky and his maker
his lone plea for help.

In the heart of wealth, he chose as his shelter this part
of the city, where upper-class snubs did not give an ear to

the cries and the songs of the weary.

Yet, I sleep and wake up every morning at Hypodrome quarters
with the hoarse cry of the solitary lunatic in my ears.
As I wake up from bed, stretch, and yawn,
I throw open my window wide, and there he lies on a torn mat,
under the shelter of the baobab tree, with both arms,
clasped behind his dreadlocked hair.
Abruptly, he gets up and engages in a frenzied solo dance
where his hoarse voice sings louder and louder by the minute.

What can I do to help get depraved lunatics off the streets?
Maybe my solitary lunatic is dead by now or maybe he is still
    alive.
Who knows?*

---

* This is a true experience that I lived through in 1996 in Yaoundé shortly be-
fore my dad passed away. My bedroom window on the second floor of our home
directly overlooked the area beyond the gates, a particular tree that was home to
a lunatic at night. He used to start singing at 5:00 a.m. every morning, and that
was my wake-up call. It was just so heart-wrenching to hear this man's voice.
When I look back today, what comes to my mind is the fact that the lunatic's
outcry was only the beginning of a series of nightmares that eventually culmi-
nated in the tragic death of my father in December 1996.

October 2006
Stranger at My Door

A streak of moonlight
suddenly percolated my doorstep,
fiercely ravaged my living room,
and tore it apart right in the
middle, as turbulently as the filmy
thick, dark, velvet
curtains of the temple when Christ
breathed his last,
juxtaposing
a percussion of darkness,
mingled half on half,
with this streak of moonlight
radiating from the starry skies,
up in the heavens.

In my living room, I lay sprawled on a thick, red,
"magida" leather puff,
located adjacent to a European modeled
Phillips color TV screen; a screen that
heavily yet tenderly caressed
the glittering red carpet of my parlor's
two-bedroom apartment.

I was uneasily half asleep,
yet trapped in a whirling spiral of
an extreme anxiety that was lost in the
early darkness of a late March evening
in my neighborhood of Obili.

As usual,
the lights had just gone out
a few minutes earlier
in this part of my world,
in this city of my inhabitance,

in this gated apartment complex
where I lived;
and right in the heart of my
tiny, four-square-foot universe,
mirrored in the streak of moonlight.

Arms akimbo on both sides of my head,
I was taken completely off guard,
as a strange feeling
abruptly engulfed my spirit,
overwhelmed me, and I
resuscitated, suddenly trapped
in a trance.

My entire persona was mysteriously
caught in a glitter of moonlight
streaking through my wide open door,
as my eyes got lost in tracking the
source of this brilliance that had
invaded my privacy.

In the source of this brilliance,
emerged an image of God,
seated on the throne with a
choir of winged angels chanting the
Gloria in excelsis Deo …
The spirit of the almighty one
reverberated in my heart,
consumed my mind, and
transformed my spirit,
transcending me to the golden gates
of heaven both spiritually and mentally.

Then an angel of the Lord
tapped on my shoulder and
whispered in my ear:
"Do not knock, for your

struggles are not over yet.
Have you accomplished
your mission?
Go back and fulfill your dreams."

Then I shook so suddenly,
catapulted on the carpet on my knees,
and began to pray fervently,
for a stranger had visited my abode
in my solitary moment of
loneliness,
                darkness,
despair,
        and worries.

Yet,
be it known this day that
on that bleak March eventide,
I heard no knock on my door,
nor saw any stranger silhouetted
against the moonlight,
when lights eventually
blasted suddenly in the room
and the streak of moonlight,
that was the stranger at my door,
disappeared with the darkness.

However, I know that I transcended
spiritually into God's universe
and briefly forgot about my earthly woes,
yearnings, and agonies,
as I now contemplate on the following thought:

How long will this perennial agony
of incertitude persist in my hopeless
life of deprived ambitions, and dreams?

Did the stranger at my door,
caught in the glitter of a moonlight
streak, transform and shape my destiny?
Only time will tell.

Engulfed by Flames

A shadow in darkness,
rushing in the loudness of the howling winds,
whisked past my ears,
as I stood on a lonely mountaintop,
awaiting the Lord's call.

I was lost in myself,
lost in a shadow of doubt
that had consumed my weary soul
and imprisoned my irate mind.

Lost in memory, I waited impatiently,
bidding on the good Lord to save my sinful soul,
and deliver my spirit from its enslaved chains of bondage.

When did I lose it all?
At the golden gate?

Ah! The Golden Gate!
What lies beyond?
Does it really matter at this point in time?

Oh yes!--------the golden gate is here and now,
right where I am.
A lonely, weary soul pursuing two urgent paths,
one that leads to light, and the other that descends to the
dungeons of firestorms.

How dare I permit my weary soul to be engulfed by flames,
in the doomed pursuit of firestorms rather than light,
where the pits of evil rest for evermore.

Therefore, reflections and daily prayer be my mantle,
be my supporting pillars in times of deep despair,
for if you tear,

then am I doomed to eternal damnation;
but if you bind and stick,
only then will my weary soul defy the enticing corridors
of darkness and sin.

September 2008
My Secret Garden

On the wings of a dove
perched on an apple tree
sits my guardian angel
garbed in white,
meticulously watching
over me.

There sits my little girl, Ameline,
on the foot of the tree,
idly picking on the brown spring
leaves wrestling with the force of
its speed at her feet.

With
melodious wind songs
whispering in the trees,
she tilts her head into
her right palm supporting
her jawline and listens
keenly with a rapacious low
hum to the rustling of the leaves
that tenderly embrace her legs,
and whip against the tree bark
forcefully jerking away in
light, speedy whispers
to recycle its sequential drumbeat.

A peaceful feeling overwhelms me
so suddenly as I feel a warm presence
in my midst,
so spiritual, yet invisible to my eyes

For a memory felt, on the foot of
an apple tree,
in the honorable presence of the dove,
symbol of God's presence, demystifies
the spiritual presence of God in our
midst, who comes to us in memory
and spirit during the most lonesome
and quiet moments of our lives;

----
if we open our hearts and lend our
presence to him, in our most secret
garden, like Ameline's.

Brandon's Evening Prayer with Mommy

Jesus, you love me,
Jesus, I love you.
You are in my heart,
and,
I am in your heart.

Summer–July 2008
Brandon's Prayer to the Soldiers at Virginia's Arlington Memorial

Sunday's mass at St. Mary's is now over
at 1:00 a.m. in the afternoon.
With Gabriel stuffing a dollar in the
charity box and lighting a candle for
grand-daddy
I stuff a dollar in the box, my turn,
and light a candle for the fallen soldiers at
Arlington Memorial, whose
park I visited Saturday on the Zohery tour bus
with Gabriel, Belal, and Nadia,
accompanied by our mums and dads,
recalling in my mind an array of
white headstones that blurred my vision,
like the confused blur of death's reality
on the battle field, unknown to a six-year-old my age.

So, when mum asks me at the west wing of the altar,
"Brandon, what do you think will happen to the souls of the
soldiers buried at Arlington Memorial?"

I, with a slight laughter and a child's playful
ignorance, flip my fingers in my mouth and
blurt out:
"I want God to keep them safe,"
as the power of that statement sinks deep in mum's mind.

Then I bow my head in wonder to ask mum the following question:

"Are the souls of the soldiers dwelling safely in heaven, mum?"

Part III: Love and Relationships: A True Vision of Life

To love is to live, and to live is to love.

Gypsy Horse Rider

I hate the despicable fury on your
ruggedly handsome face.
It rags my nerves
and tears it into wanton pieces of
lustful desire raging in my brains.

Cupid's arrow of love must strike your heart,
so like the goddess of love,
your furious emotions
need to experience that magical turmoil
that has enslaved my heart,
and rendered you the object of my affection.

Your brooding, dark, gypsy looks,
reminiscent of your wild, horse,
caravan life,
lived through the ages of time,
against an unknown backdrop
of heir apparent to a wealthy, vast estate
bares the daredevil in you.

Yet, a noble lady of the upper-class
I am, but your gypsy birth beneath mine
is an offensive deterrent to stratified barriers
matching betrothals, class to class, which are
reflections of revolutionary ideals.

Cupid's magical arrow of love then
renders the object of my affection
heir apparent to the throne.

So is the fury in your eyes all gone?

So will my gypsy horse rider embrace that
magical turmoil which enslaves my heart,

lest on the proud wings of Cupid's love,
we nest together through an ageless
age of timeless time.

Goddess in the Mirror

A gigantic, golden, artistic piece
of gorgeous Aphrodite Pandemos
planted in the main lobby of the
Madrigal hotel.

The receptionist, already accustomed
to her decorous presence, comfortably leans on
a cushioned seat behind a green marble
 furnished desk, in great anticipation
for an exhilarating evening to commence.

Intoxicated by the smell of cigars, and wine, blended
with a sophisticated mélange of perfumes, inhaled
from incoming limousine customers, the receptionist
drowsily welcomes all with a charming smile
fit for a Buckingham princess.

Her imposing demeanor as she overlooks the
huge wall mirror to the left of the room is a
majestic bonanza for excited bambinos ready to
gamble on the massive roller-coaster roulettes.

The customers walk into the room arm in arm,
with talon high, *rouge-a-levre bordels**
stringed on their arms in semi-conscious moods
of obscene, wine-drugged stupor.

Yet, the receptionist continues to attend to her guests
with a warm-hearted feeling of ease.
She entertains them with background robotic
rhythms of blues that dominantly captivate the
romantic aroma of a dimly lit, multicolored room,
leathered with fashionable, cream-white, Italian sofas.

----

*red-lipsticked prostitutes

So do lovers here snuggle into each other in
amorous whispers, with love tenderly mirrored in the
starry glitter of their enigmatic eyes, caught in the flickering
candlelit flames of the goddess in the mirror.

So too, can everyone read the bold inscription on
her lips, engraved in metallic, gold letters
which chime:

"*Welcome ...*"
and invitingly continues in bolder gold carvings to her
chest:

"*To Madrigal Hotel. Dine; sup; gamble;* and *dance
with me tonight.*"

Midnight Silhouette

Her name was Idelda.
But the villagers and grandmothers
called her Ideili … yaiyi … dil, as she walked
with her leopard sandals, just like a leopard
ready to bask in the sun.
She was a budding fourteen year old, and when
ever the sun shone, she looked like a rose flower,
ready to be nipped at the bud.
But, she was a forbidden fruit that sprouted from an
unknown womb.

On this eventful night, when manhood was celebrated
in the open arena, she gracefully stole the show as:

Poised like an African model
on this romantic, midnight, lover's lane,
I could see her all!
Glittering like gold,
but as dark as moonless midnight
on this late November evening,
as I stood dumbstruck
at the crowded village arena of
Kikwini's triangular crossroads.

She was standing on her toes,
with her arms curved in, gently
swaying to the tune of the samba.

Her imposing demeanor was matchless
against that of her peers, who looked like
impostors planted in a circle of frenzied
ritualistic dance.

With a single wrapper tied above her busty breasts;

some cowries and laced bracelets banded around her forehead;
and rich creamy pearls strung on her neck, waistline
and ankles;
she was a fiery feast for lecherous eyes prowling the
arena grounds with hungry tiger eyes.

Breathless,

the spectators watched.
Such beauty and splendor of yesteryears,
the villagers had not beheld;
Such refined, ebony smoothness, in the likes of
Nakuma, the attractive palace princess was a rarity
to perceive, in the twinkle of an eye,
in this tribal community of my youth;

For in her clear amber eyes
could be seen sparkling,
the wild exotic excitement
that such teenage youthfulness
possessed;
As her glaring beauty uniquely stood out
in this shadowed circle of moonlit,
frenzied, midnight, ritual dancers
tapping their jangly, bangly, feet
to the rhythmic beat of the Njang Fubuh.*

So, like the spring roses that blossom and sprout
in the beauty of multiple, fascinating colors,
then wither and die in the windy harshness
of fall's fall, would such a blossomed rose ever wither?

Njang Fubuh   The "Njang" is a type of traditional dance performed by
women from the Kom tribe in the northwest area of Cameroon.

B
    E
        H
           O
              L
                  D,

My thoughts so suddenly swayed!
That breathtaking moment,
that magical, ethereal beauty
is but a privileged stage in life,
which blossoms and then withers
with age;

So,
as we journey on through life's thorny path,
memories come and go,
so too are the patterned days of our lives,

For didn't each and every one of us once blossom
like a moonlight silhouette caught in the drama
of a frenzied, midnight, ritualistic dance similar to Idelda's?

Drumbeats of Medieval Lifestyle

One Saturday evening,
during winter's January,
 in Las Vegas,

My husband and I were riding on a passenger tram,
        from Excalibur to Luxor,
when the luxuries of man's medieval architectural invention
        glittered before my eyes in golden flashes of
visible monumental proportion, reflected in the
        Arthurian legendary lifestyle of fifteenth-century King Arthur,
and the medieval Celtic knights of the round table.

The passengers on the tram looked very serious,
        and chatted not too easily.
Each was rushing to the casinos that blasted life
        into the different platforms of regular day-to-day gambling
at this Las Vegas resort in contrast to the solemn royalty and
reverence
        that surrounded King Arthur, and his legion of sworn
knights
at the round table mural, overlooking the gamblers.
        Were we also there for the gambling at the casinos?

When we dropped off the tram,
        we strolled into the glittery sophistications of the connect
between the two hotels.

Carpets that linked both hotels were designed
        in deep, rich colors of red, and golden brown,
billboards of magnificent proportion, advertising
        the latest Hollywood movies on the side walls of
moving escalators, accompanied by rhythmic
        rhythms of hard rock, mingled with jazz and blues,
ignited the airwaves, and roughened my senses
        to the beauty and pleasure of life's luxuries.

Taking souvenir photos, sneaking past wedding chapels,
 descending and ascending escalators,
life in this part of the world,
 after midnight, just like daylight, was still booming.

Stupefied, I entered the tomb of Nebuchadnezzar, one of
the powerful kings of Egypt's ancient historical
times, and oh! did I just surface in a world that mirrored the
life and times of ancient kings?

Yet, that was not the end of my adventure in this city
 of flickering dreams,
  as
a tantalizing performance of *Mamma Mia* in one of the
 theaters, only increased my appetite to explore a
 hotel named after the sword of King Arthur.

Then,
lavished images of King Arthur sitting at a round table
 with loyal knights, flashed on a mural at the suite
entrance, in a fashionable exhibit of refined class consciousness.

Lodged at the hotel for a conference,
 we were part of a diversified team of conferences.

The overwhelming beauty of the hotels attracted much attention
 from tourists and locals.
It reminded me of what the conference host said in a welcome
address: "What happens in Vegas stays in Vegas."

So folks, when you visit Las Vegas next time,
 enjoy;

the beauty of the palm trees,
 the delicious taste of American and Mexican appetizing
delicacies,

the movies and theatrical performances of seasoned actors and
actresses,
the glittering billboards on the street hyperbolizing the latest
        movies,
 musical performances in town,
        the golden view of the city that overlooks your hotel room's
window in glittering lights of magical dramatization;

        then,
put money in your pocket and engage in the sophisticated,
        jamboree lifestyle of gambling on the assorted tables of
billionaire winners and losers;
        drink to your fill,
and with that brown cigar, dangling at the tip of your lips,
        stay sober and win the game,
rather than lose with the wink of an eye at the seducing waitresses
in red mini-dresses,
        who scurry from table to table, serving drinks to casino
gamblers.

In all, folks,
put money in your pocket, because
no money,
no game,

and,

no game,
no money

So,

welcome to Las Vegas, the land of dreams and opportunity;

But,

be warned, lest you leave the city, and carry your casino
dreams with you, for indeed;

"What happens in Las Vegas stays in Las Vegas."

So, folks,
visit the Excalibur hotel in Las Vegas,
and dream the night away, medieval yet casino style,
with today's modern knights of the round table,
visible in murals adorning its walls.*

---

*   Is the casino lifestyle at the Excalibur a heroic reminiscence of the lifestyle
of twelfth-century Celtic knights like King Arthur and the Knights of the Round
Table? If it is, then where are the live horses, the swords, the garments, the mys-
terious round table, and the huge castles? Your five senses will unfold this magi-
cal phenomenon in the huge architectural mural placed on the top wall overlook-
ing a suite entrance in the east wing of Las Vegas's Excalibur hotel. In 2007, my
husband and I stayed at the Excalibur hotel in Las Vegas for a few days while he
attended a conference.

January 2000
Millennium Fireworks

What did I know about loneliness?
It was but two years ago that you abandoned
and left me at the mercy of crack jungle wolves
to rot and die without a penny.

Homeless, penniless, abandoned, and deserted,
I walked the crowded streets of downtown Manhattan
on a busy, wintry Saturday evening, begging for a dime
and a shelter to lay my weary head and rest.

Little did I know then that it was the dawn of a
new millennium,
for the drugs had numbed my brains and I had
dark, gaping holes where pretty teeth once lurked.
Who could I turn to? Who could I talk to?

Was I not the scum of society's remnant leftover,
that had lost its foothold, waiting for death to
relieve me of passing ghostly shadows that daily
tormented my mind and drove me crazy,
reminding me of heavenly days long lost in a
despicable act of humanity called divorce?

However,
it is now the dawn of a new millennium and the
numbness in my brain is wearing off.
Is life worth living?
Like the seasons, I have weathered the storm
and now, I am regenerating like the spring leaves.

At the dawn of a new millennium, here I stand
lost in the multitude of crowds gathered at
Times Square in downtown New York.

With millennial balloons flying high and
live artists performing on stage, crowds
of tourists and New Yorkers gyrate to the musical
beat of pop music blasting the airwaves.
Fireworks in display, explode to the midnight
maddening countdown to 12:00 a.m.
at the drop of the fireball.

It is a new year, and a new day;
Excitement trumpets the airwaves and
television screens worldwide project
young lovers and old lovers,
families and friends,
tourists and nationals,
all hugging and kissing,
crying and laughing,
screaming and yelling, and thankful to the Lord for having survived
a new millennium.
Who wouldn't be?

In my raggy-taggy, I have shed my oldies mentally.
A broad smile on my face, I have defied man's woes.
As a new person and a new being, I now cross the street
heading toward the nearest rehabilitation ward
to seek help.

Who says millennium fireworks aren't an inspiration,
a window to a world of despair that resurges dead
emotions, and old desires of yesteryears?

So, with the musical beat of pop still in
the airwaves, I think that life is worth living,
but will society embrace a druggy lunatic who once
walked the crowded streets of downtown Manhattan
lost in the passage of time at the beginning of a new millennium?
I know not.

All I know is that the millennial fireworks have ignited
a wild passion in me, to grab life with a fierceness
not yet beheld by man, and not to let go.

Only then will my delicate emblem of faith flicker into a firework
of hope;
So too will my driven zeal for life as I survive the tide resurge on
this
 passionate winter eventide, while I walk the crowded streets of
New York's Times Square lost in memory.

Passionate Encounter

With a detached air of passionate nuance,
he was seated in a dimly lit corner of the
swim club with just his swimsuit on,
gently perusing the pages of a men's journal

Suddenly, he lifted his fiery green eyes and started
glimpsing around the room with a detached air
of jaded, mingled mischief,
as on stage,
the minstrel's deep, rasping voice towered over
the microphone and vibrated a lovely romantic tune
meant for lovers.

Could this spectacle of boredom be fine-tuned
into an unexpected encounter destined to happen?

The hustle and bustle of the crowded room did not
affect him nor his distant thoughts in any way.

Seated on a candlelit table at the opposite end of the room,
I just couldn't take my eyes off this Adonis as I
celebrated my eighteenth birthday with mum at this enticing
resort. A sudden creepy feeling overwhelmed me, and
I stared right across the room.

Then it happened …
He stared at me, and I stared at him.
Green and jet black collided in midair and exploded
into tiny pieces of glass, juxtaposing sweet and sour fireworks.
Distant memories invaded my instant thoughts, and possessed
my fiery mind gone wild with desire.

My heart started racing, racing like an athlete in a hundred-
meter marathon.
It started racing to grab something, something that I could
not figure out at that moment, as his possessive eyes
consumed my entire being, focused on my features, lingered there,
then up to my eyes again to passionately possess me.
I lost my foothold and dropped my eyes, suddenly pulling back
my seat and rushing out into the cool, calm, summer air,
as the minstrel's romantic beat faded through the revolving
glass doors.

I needed some fresh air.
Without realizing I had been running, I found myself
amongst some thick green shrubs within the garden of the pool.
Then my mind raced back to a point in time!

Could he be the one?

Could he be the one who had been invading my dreams
dressed as a marine in the navy, ready to set sail for war
in the terrorist-infested caves of Afghanistan's rocky mountains?
Could I be tamed by such a sailor whose encounter with
rustic pirates in the high seas had molded his spirit
and challenged his strength?

Could he be the one with rich, raven-black hair, and sea green eyes,
whom I visualized in shadows of my teenage dreams?
Could he be the one recently returned from Operation
Desert Storm, to storm, then catapult my own world
of romantic dreams?

Could he invade my heart and weaken my resolve
to resist such fiery, attractive men at eighteen,
or could it be that I was just a young, passionate, naïve
fool who was simply infatuated with an Adonis whose possessive
eyes
and enticing lips brazenly seduced me under the translucency of
dim multicolored lights that pitched into shades of darkness
surrounding him in such a romantic place?

Yet again, I could feel the creeps on the back of my neck,
as if someone was watching me.
Then I heard a creaky noise and a hoarse voice
whisper in my ear,
"Do not be afraid and do not move,"
as I jumped sideward, terrified, and collided chest on
with bottomless, deep, Pacific, sea green eyes staring at me
like a shark ready to pounce.

With my heartbeat accelerating, then pounding in my ears,
I turned so sharply all fists out, ready to punch!

Mighty fists grabbed my tiny little arms as once more,
bottomless sea green eyes rapidly possessed jet black.
Then, I started reeling and losing my foothold,
as my knees buckled, and I succumbed effortlessly
in the arms of a massive brick wall fiercely gripping me.

Then he possessed my lips, and I lost total control of my senses.

Was I falling in love, or was I already madly in love with a
stranger?

Tender Is the Moon

Tender is the moon that stares brazenly from the night sky,
sucking in the breath of a still, night air, whispering deep,
throaty songs of love to the mass of earth that lies beyond its
smoldering glare.

With rooftops that light up the night sky, images of shadows
sized in Ping-Pong balls spread its breath on rooftops,
attracting the fairy tales of love.

Visions of lovers dancing in a ballroom permeate the coolness
of a romantic night sky as they clutch each other and rush to
a hidden maze under the stars of a palazzo garden to steal
dreamy kisses.

So as the tender moon embraces the darkness that lights up the
       night
sky, starry glitters fall on lovers again hugging tightly in deserted
       lanes
void of predators.

They tell dreamy stories of long wars battled in dangerous lands
far from home as they return from war to resume normal life.

But memories of heroic ventures on daring battlefields resurge
and capture their imagination as they cling to their loved ones,
afraid, lest they be snatched by dark visions of deadly encounters
rife in their memories and daily nightmares.

As they tremble to the chill of the softly whispering winds
       caressing
their hair, they cling to each other, bonding and healing tenderly,
like the moon, their differences emanating from long years of
separation.

So as the tender moon mingles with the stars that nip at its bud to generate twinkles that float through the darkness in glitters telescoped in the lover's eyeball, a sign of hope renders promises of joy in the wings of the invincible dove that hovers over their heads and guards against any future trepidations that may dare to mar their happiness, as the tender moon joins in the bliss.

Stranger at the Bar

From outside the bar I came, into the bar I strolled,
as moody as the sunset that dimed the grey clouds
overhead.
With my yellow tank top worn above my skinny
dark LEVI jeans, I threw a black leather jacket over
my shoulders and stumbled in …

He was seated on a bar stool, taking a shot of scotch
whiskey.
His short, black, and wavy hair attractively shaped
      the contours of a hard muscled handsome face
           that instantly drew my curiosity and attention.

He saw me in the crowd and stared brazenly
into my eyes.
I blinked in shock, for I had not seen a face, so handsome
in my teenage years.
He winked at me in amusement, and his luminous eyes
      blurred into a dark brooding look, with eyebrows
           creased together, in pensive thought.

I knew him not.
He knew me not.
For we were strangers at a bar, staring brazenly
at each other,
      ready to jump into each other's arms,
           embrace, and kiss wildly.

But I knew him not,
and, he knew me not,
for, we were strangers at a bar, staring brazenly
at each other,
while the clouds descended behind the dark brooding
hills of Beverly,
      and the guard at the post stood with his gun

pointing up the sky,
   ready to guard visitors at the Bay restaurant,
myself, included.

Who should make the first move?

Then I looked around me and saw a sea of faces eating and
chatting loudly.
I saw ten uniformed marines with their beautiful wives
 and children, eating dinner cozily.

A waitress walked up to me and as she began to walk me
 to a table, the stranger made a move in my direction,
 whispered something in the ear of one of the marines,
and I got lost again in the crowd.

Later, when I lifted my eyes and looked around me,
the stranger at the bar was no where to be seen.

A few seconds later, he stood before me, with his arms
folded on his chest, staring brazenly into my eyes again
as he asked:
"Would you be my Valentine on this night of February
 the 14th?"

To Mommy with Love

I sat on my mom's lap
I said look!
I see a cloud shape like a dog.
I love sitting on my mom's lap.
                    Love, Brandon

I love my mom.

January 1, 2000
Memories

Vivid memories never die.

They blossom in my mind
like a lovely white rose
of a loved one long gone,
separated by oceans across
the Mediterranean Sea.

Wild desires stir my senses
to a point of blind obsession
as I no longer think of any
but my dearly beloved in a
distant land; dare to recall
family life together

My heart cries out in misery
silently praying for the days
to speed up!
Alas! as slow as a snail, they drag on,
bringing this melancholic sigh to my lips,

Reminding me of days long gone
when blissful happiness though
torn by obstacles unperceived,
bonded us together like a magnet
through all the thorny paths that
we trotted in our youthful years
of struggle, with patience the key word.

Yet memories refreshed, it is a new year and a new
beginning.
From the dream city of Munich's Marian Platz,
 to the land of freedom at this moment,

though oceans across the high seas still separate us,
we may as well join the marathon that races us
to the mountain top of millennial celebrations on
this lonely midnight of New Year's Eve, as I gaze
endlessly at the television screen.

The Rose (To My LESAN Sisters)

My alma mater is like a red, red, red, red rose that blossoms
in the sunshine of a fresh spring morning, basking
in the star-studded gem of its richness.

Back in time, we breathed the freshness of its early morning
rise at the clang of the bell that woke us up at 5:00 a.m.
to shower and head to early morning mass at the cathedral.

Then, weary and tired, yet refreshed and yawning, we would
flock like sheep down the winding hill, sleepy still from the
previous day's campus chores.

Replicas of the colors of green, red, yellow, and blue
counterpanes that hug the array of beds in the dorms,
would replace the anxious feet that parade its floors
in a hustle and in a bustle.

Then smell of the honeybee sucking on the nectar of the
roses on the flower beds at the early rise of sunshine would
perfume our nostrils, mingled with the catalysts of butter,
jam, peanut butter, and chocolate spread on French bread
as we rush down the steps of the refectory after breakfast.

Then we would feel the richness of the redness of our red skirts,
as it whirls and caresses our legs, while we hustle around campus
all day, supported by the creaminess of the blouses that starkly
generate the glitter and laughter in our glorious, youthful eyes.

Such were our good old days in Our Lady of Lourdes, now distant
yet vivid memories of a past that richly brands like tattoos images
of our precious lives, reaped from the fruits that we sowed then,
and passed on to the younger generation.

So, as the redness of the rose immortalizes its freshness, born to a
LESAN sister, so too will the seeds multiply and beget new roses
in the spin of gyres.

Proud to be a LESAN

Our Alma Mater,
Is the sweetest thing that be.
We have traversed oceans and strange lands,
to graciously come together as a unified whole,
bred of innocence and humility in this land of plenty.

We have gathered the fold, and the gold, and materialized
projects into swift actions that have generated springs
tunneled to the attractive gems that still inhabit the campus
of our alma mater.

We have uplifted the spirits of the needy in desperate
moments of need, when all hope was lost and
weary feet that usually trotted to the valley
of disease and death, with haunted looks in their eyes
have materialized into Canaan miracles, fulfilled by the
unyielding dedication of committed sisters in Christ.

Together, we have marched like gigantic warriors
to brave challenges, and differences, true only to
human nature.
We have laid a solid foundation,
built a strong and courageous union,
moved mountains, conquered obstacles,
and served humanity to the best of our ability.

We have and will continue this servitude and
commitment to a proud Catholic institution that has injected
    morals, dedication, commitment, respect, and
humility to our fold.
So are we blessed and humbled by the presence
of the invisible one who always hovers in our midst.

So who would not be proud of an institution like ours
that has bred lawyers, doctors, teachers, pilots, Wall

Street magnates, politicians, and all?

Therefore, tighten your belts LESAN sisters, and dance
to the beat of the "dombolo," without ceasing to pray, and thank
God for the sweet gems, who will become future gold mines
of LESA, so generations will keep the torchlight burning with
an everlasting flame of peace and love,
rekindled in the hearts of one and all in our alma mater.

Through My Eyes (Stories from the Heart)

There is a lone star in the sky that only my eyes can see.
Then an airplane with its lights pitched against the dark
night sky rumbles by with a thunderous loud noise,
killing the calmness of the atmosphere.

The airplane is millions of miles away from this lone star,
yet the common link that binds them is their brightness in
darkness.

At the end of a busy workday, residents' cars fill the
parking lot of Elverson village apartments at this time
of the night.
Brandon seated on my lap on the main stairs of the
entrance overlooking the parking lot points to the
still night sky with his little wet fingers just out of his
mouth and screams:
"Mommy, look! I can see an airplane!"
Then a few minutes later, he excitedly
screams again:
"Mommy, look! There is thunder."
Then I ask him, "Where is the thunder, baby?"
Then he shouts:
"The thunder is in the trees-s-s-s, Mommy!"
Then I laugh, and he laughs and adds again:
"Mommy, look! The thunder is in the sky-y-y-y!"

There is neither thunder in the trees nor in the sky,
on this hot summer evening when the sun has
already retreated from the sky to be replaced by
fathomless, piercing stars randomly displayed against
the backdrop of a communion-shaped half moon.
But the parking lot is swamped with trees and cars.
Then we both laugh and laugh until our eyes are
wet with tears.

Then I ask him,
"Baby, can you give your mommy one big hug?"
He giggles and fiercely grabs my neck with both arms,
floods my face with sweet, dreamy kisses,
and screams; "I love you, Mommy!"
Fiercely, I also hug him too and reply;
"I love you too, baby boy Brandon!"

Cozily, he snuggles into my arms and falls asleep quietly,
as I keep staring at the lone, bright star,
lost in the shadows of the pitch-dark sky.
The thunderous noise of the airplane has already faded
into the distant skies by now as reality sets in again.

On this silent, cool, calm, breezy, and very romantic
night, I sit outside on the entrance stairs of Elverson
apartments with my two-year-old son, Brandon,
listening to his chuckles and basking in the beauty of
a refreshing, starry night sky.
Amazingly, he has just vividly visualized the world
through the innocent eyes of a two-year-old.

Then, the double glass doors open, and
my husband steps outside with a Malta in hand, smiling.
Sitting down next to me, he kisses the baby,
leans on my shoulder, and we all bask in this
blissful, romantic happiness that bonds us as a family,
with a great and mighty hug, reflected in the
starry night sky.

Isn't it such fun
to often mirror the world
through the shadowy eyes of a two-year-old
on a cozy June evening such as this?

In Those Days

I would sit on my mother's lap
Commanding the world to come to me
I would whimper, and twist, and turn, and yell
just to focus attention on me, angered by
incessant conversations between mum and dad
that drove my tiny little brains crazy.

I wish they could read my innocent mind
that had neither the power of speech yet
nor could even identify objects on the wall,
symbols of nothing in my eyes.
What did I know about colors, objects, and people?
Visions scanned in my mind's eye all day long!

Then Kiki and Mimi would come rushing into the room
with the wind at their backs, kicking, and yelling, and
punching, and screaming, loud enough for the walls to
collapse.

Conversations would abruptly come to a standstill,
and I would smile that bittersweet smile of relief,
not because I had regained their attention but
because mum, distracted, would tenderly drop me
on the carpet to trot around with my tiny little feet
and hands to continue my daily mischievous rampage.

Such were my childhood years,
which are but bittersweet memories now.

Tribute to My Mother

You left me when I was a child
and,
returned when I was a grown woman
with breasts on my chest and womanhood
in my body.

You understood me not for a long while
and
I understood you not for a long while.
Confused I was—yes—of life's tedious
complications in understanding the
simple things of life that a loving
mother would teach her daughter.

Bonds we broke and mended like shoes, the
pieces of our lives through the lengthy years
of my adolescence and twenties when I often
strolled and meditated through the silent streets
of Bastos, and Hippodrome.

But in the end, as I whirl time in oblivion,
and ponder over the years of my adolescence
into womanhood, I have often felt remorse over our
life together and wondered why I did what I did,
or
why you did what you did.

For the chronic habits of life's past have a way of
stealthily creeping into the present in ways that
are unknown to us, because we shed off the old
habits and adapt to new ways of mirroring life
through the mirage of our shadows that chase us
into an old age, reflected in our past.

But I say to you now from the past to the present and

forever that I have always loved you, Mom.
For if you were not there to give me the features
of my long nose, reminiscent of my grandmother Anna-Veronica's,
often labeled on me as I walk the crowded streets of cities, and
taught me the ways that lead to heaven, how will I be who I am
today?

Oh! my mother, God has reminded me that,
gush! I can only have one mother, love one mother, and cherish
with love all the sacrifices she has made to raise me.
For that I am so grateful, thus none other than you has trotted with
me through the battlefield of inexperience during my immature
years,
as we have soaked wet our tears and drenched them on each other's
shoulders, ready to journey together through God's amazing grace.

So now is the time for us to celebrate our lives, and years together,
for what you said to me,
you said it right, Mom,
what you taught me,
you taught it right, Mom,
what you chastised me for,
you did so right, Mom,
and what you dreamed of your daughter's future,
you did so right, Mom,
and my love for you has only grown stronger over the years,
for who is a perfect human being anyway?

Tell me one if you find one, for I doubt if you might
ever find one as you stampede your way through life's
perennial journey in search of a mother's love.

The Storm in Her Eyes

Shrouded in irresistible beauty and elegance,
her innocence was like a leaf
that raindrops could not penetrate,
no matter how hard the bouncer boys
who were drawn to her like bees to nectar
teased.

She was a mystery to behold, behind that
veiled barricade, that netted the deep,
lost, penetrating gaze of unpredictable,
sea blue eyes which mesmerized her admirers,
and plunged them into the depths of
a stormy blue sea, chasing wild sharks.

She used it as a shield to wade young
naughtiness off,
while hiding her tangle of voluptuous
honey gold hair in a hijab.

She rejected male stares by always
looking down, as if she had something to hide
but the curious guys would not let her
be her real self for once.

So, she erected a vigilant barricade within
her anonymous self by vowing to a
strict code of silence, and no improper
conduct

Mute, she became such a quiet nuisance that
none could tolerate her weirdness,
for,
she alone knew the secret to her
awkward behavior.

Part IV: Secular: A Vision of Routine Life

"Life is a circus, and man is a player in the center"

I Dream

I am just a little Bulu kid of thirteen,
and yet I dream …

Wearing a faded yellow soccer T-shirt,
bought from a popular thrift store in my
soccer-obsessed neighborhood of Essos,
I walk down the street into the gates of
Omnisport stadium's soccer field
with my teammates, ready for daily
inter-quarter soccer, and amateur practice, with lots of
anxiety churning my hungry stomach.
The field is muddy, grassless, dirty, and abandoned,
yet I cling on to my dream, by not giving up
the practice.

Yet, the hype in the match when ever it begins
with Coach Mbarga, supersedes the filthiness of my
surroundings as nothing, nothing indeed!
becomes more important than the latest football coach
who is looking for young players to recruit into
division one and two teams.

And this, all the more, is the reason why I dream _____!

I see you, Biloa, every afternoon on my way home from
Bilingual High School Essos, and I wonder: Why are you not
sitting in a classroom? ---------- at age thirteen?

I, Biloa, see the players in the national team play the
African Nation's Cup, then, the World Cup,
and in my haste to beat the odds of poverty,
that grimly surround my parents' financial status,
I tackle the ball with my bare feet, for my sneakers
are all worn and torn, yet with no money to buy new ones,
I fervently hold on to my dreams.

With Mvondo, Assana, Bikok, Bipum, and I, these are
dreams that for other young footballers of my status
have ardently materialized with prestigious selections into
the junior lions, and that exactly is why I dream too, Papito.

So, on your way home from Paris, Papito,
I ask nothing from you, big bro,
but money to buy me some sneakers to tackle, and play
my soccer game.

As an everyday spectator outside the Omnisport stadium,
I see the dream in his eyes, I see the talent in his feet,
the strength in his moves, and the strong conviction in
his persona, to pursue his dreams.

So, I, Biloa, dream big, and think big, and play big, and hope
that one day,
I will be an Indomitable Lion, so I can score goals and make
my country proud;
and one day,
I will be solicited by a prominent European soccer team,
to prove my worth;
since my inspirational ticket to this world of fleeting dreams is my
most famous star, labeled on my soccer T-shirt,
Samuel Eto'o Fils,
who plays millions of miles away from home,
in the Italian Serie A club, Internazionale.

Yet, I dream, …
for he is my African hero …

Challenges

Raging winds of Hurricane
Solomon angrily yank my rooftop.
A whirlwind of confusion
spiraling in the air,
traps me in a raging blizzard
as stockpiles of debris
litter Green Wood Street, and
residues from valued property float down my neighborhood.

A daredevil you are!
How do I sort myself out?

Episodes of Loneliness

The grass was so lonely that it began to scream.
I could hear its screaming in tiny whistling motions
that swayed it left, then right, in an effortless plea
for help.

I could not understand why it was so restless.
So I decided to tread on its innocence.

What I discovered blew my mind to the vineyard.

The beginning of fall had set it on edge,
For it had started mourning the loss of its greenery.
The abandoned cypress trees were just dishing out chunks of
branch pieces on its floor as this was ruining its beauty;

To further upset it,

Fall weather had just set in, and the cypress trees readied to splash
its
floor with red, yellow, and brown leaves.

No human soul had dared to notice the filthiness of its floors,
nor acknowledge even that it was uncomfortable and even more so,
abandoned.

It was typically reminded of the vineyard grass that was so blessed.
For the grass at the vineyard was regularly mowed and cleaned.
It had a company of assorted
Green, yellow, and red apples;
Green, yellow, and pink grapes;
Blue, black, and red grapefruits;
Green and yellow bananas;
Green and yellow mangoes;
Brown, black, and green pears;
Yellow peaches;

And all these pieces of natural loveliness
were planted on the vineyard in contrast to
the abandoned cypress trees that limply and scantily stared at the
lonely grass.

Moreover, the boozing noise of construction that overlooked the
MLK
scarcely noticed its plea for quietness.

Then, at that moment in time, Jason, standing at the parking lot,
suddenly shouted to Amelia, standing at the main entrance of
the building:
"Hi, Amelie! Can I trespass on this lonely grass and come give
you a hug,
for the grass is so lonely that it yearns for company!"

The Incomplete of Me

Is dramatized in my attitude.
Wearing a ruffled black wool coat,
with pockets entrenched to
its sides, I keep my gloved fingers inside
as I uneasily parade up and
down the sidewalk of Sunset Boulevard
with tall, knee-high boots on.

Looking tall and elegant, my rich, thick,
chocolate, dark hair streams slightly
beyond my shoulders as the chilly winds
wisp it back and forth against my blushed cheeks.
My mind is flooded with anxiety, longing,
and a terrible sense of loneliness.

What exactly am I longing for?
So,
up and down the street I briskly walk
on this cold, chilly January evening
puffing a cigarette, downed to the butt,
just to keep my body warm.

With my coat collar raised above my ears,
a white limousine suddenly pulls up besides
the sidewalk,
and the impressive driver hastily beckons,
"Hey, ma'am, looking for company?"
Here's one, pointing to the backseat.

The ruggedly handsome face that stares at me
from the tinted windshield has on
a tailored dark suit, matching an impeccable
white shirt, knotted with a crisp, silky, red bowtie.
He smiles, and I too smile.

He beckons me with his finger,
taps the seat next to him, and
invites me to hop in!

There I go! -----------------
Hopping into a strange limousine with
an absolute stranger.
Destination? Unknown!

But I sigh with a deep sense of trepidation,
then relief,
for I would have something to eat
on my plate,
after a day's work, earned on the
streets.

But where did I go wrong?

Sold at the age of seven on the streets
to a drug trafficker,
I was bought to serve as a nanny
and not get trapped in the violent
dorms of maniacs living life by destroying life.
Such was the story told!

Escape from the resort
to the lurking dark streets becomes my obsession.
I defy the terror by manipulating
its tactics, as I now sit staring at the handsome
stranger, cozily chatting with me.

Where then did my parents go wrong?

The Lost Pearl

I am a lost pearl at the bottom of a stormy sea,
with my thoughts stretched deep into the recesses
of my mind.

I find myself tipping over then sinking deep
to grasp the tightly entangled pearl swaying
with tides that rough up the sea waves on the
surface, then chase anxious surfers back to the
shore.

The anxious surfers wait for the dangerous tides
to recede so they can continue their sport, but will
the surfers discover the tightly entangled pearl lost
at the bottom of the sea?

Though low spirited, my soul yearns for
something, something I cannot have now,
but will I have it when I disentangle and retrieve
the pearl from unsteady tides that have attempted
to rip me to pieces and blur my vision?

Only time will tell …

Thinking Inside the Box

Is a fallacious conservative appeal
that stifles human progress and reveals a lot
about your personality.

So,
you need to stop thinking inside the box
and let loose your mind,
So the wind will kite it like the birds and
grapple with the ambitious dreams that
have capped your very own existence
from the day that you were born.

You need not stifle your luck and key it
in a Pandora's box,
Nor need you squash the talent and ambitions
of those you meet in your tedious journey through
a life whose sublime vision has been
limited to the fanciful pursuit of your own sublunary
dreams marred by an obstinate grasp on a single
thread that can either stretch too thin or expand
too wide.

Hold on to your dreams like open windows that
cry freedom to the world and strive not to
impose discord but instill harmony where it is
needed.

Therefore,
be not a symbol of discord but one of harmony
that breathes liberty, choice, and amalgamation
into a life that functions by thinking outside the box.

Fanatic Fallacies

Ignorant minds breed dangerous minds.
Intelligent minds breed creative minds
in a civilized society like ours.

However,
in case there is a dramatic shift from the
ignorant
                to the
                        intelligent,
incessant shadows of guilt will otherwise,
instantly tend to propel us toward the former,
whose ambiguous lifestyle is fed by dangerous
ideological fantasies, bred and nurtured in institutions
by autocrats, who rise from the hidden shadows
of civilized society to strike deadly vicious, when opportune.

But, if
intelligence conquers ignorance, then the dove will breed angels of
rage
to conquer the Armageddon of insanity,
through the power of apocalyptic tongues
raging in the prophetic curse of Sodom and Gomorrah.

Incidents of Color

I was riding in the U-Bahn one cold spring morning
from city to city,
when I sat on a seat and felt like a total stranger,
who had violated the rights of a tall, blond, young lady,
rushing to work in the morning's rush hour.

She sat beside me, opened wide her newspaper, and stuck it
above her nose, pretending to read, yet I knew she was not reading.
I bent my head and felt a peculiar discomfort.

So, I raised my eyes, and peeking on the side,
I saw a mighty frown, that burdened my heart
and made me wonder—
was my presence the object of such discontent,
manifested in attitude, yet pretentious in expression?

For darker than dark, I saw not one board,
but fairer than fair, ran skin deep.
At the exit, she rushed out so quickly. Yet, to this day,
I still do not understand the complexities that defined
her attitude.

Who should be blamed for the voiceless undertones of
stratified, racial lunacy, manifested by a stranger toward another
stranger of varying complexions and complexities that define
our world nowadays?

The Voice of Mirrors

Blanketed through my brain and emerged
in an arena of yard sales
splashed on the courtyards of the Emerson's
home complex, recently constructed with the
most sophisticated technology to accommodate
retirees, recently turned fifty-five-plus.

As our weary eyes scanned the populace of buyers
navigating the courtyard in wheelchairs and walking sticks
through the car windows,
I so suddenly saw an old white lady, strolling up the street.

On eye contact, she smiled at me, stared at the kids
in a matter of seconds, then immediately looked at me,
with curiosity in her eyes, and so I wondered,
why so curious? I contemplated, did she look at us, and pass
some casual shrug of indifference, based on the color of black
against white? Did she scorn what she saw or pity it? Or just look
at it with pure disdain?

For the voice of an old lady can so often be mirrored
in eyes that tell so many different stories of race, equation,
and balance,
as if we are mathematical problems that need to be solved,
in the parking lot of a group home.

Such are the thoughts that occupy my mind as I
watch Bella and her group perform their latest single
at the auditorium of the Emerson complex.

The Beauty of Color

On a late Sunday evening
Of October's fall,
Nadia once went to LD Nails
to shape her eyebrows.

As she advanced into the shop,
her eyes perceived the beauty
of a woman's toenails,
hoisted on the edge of a
spa pedicure tub with a
Chinese young girl, polishing
this fine specimen of fairness
with white, silky cream nail polish,
while the lady was intensely
perusing the pages of an *In Touch*
magazine.

The beauty of such polished toes
fascinated her so much that
she blinked thrice and just kept on staring
until she was beckoned to go into
the adjacent room and shape her brows.

Then as she lay on the bed, waiting for the
attendant to service her, she suddenly thought
about her own toenails, trapped in her faded
canvas shoes, and felt very ashamed.

WHY?
The fair, mulatto complexion of this woman's skin
blended so perfectly with the silky cream nail polish
on her toes.

Yet what is so amazing is often the tendency for us to
perceive in the beholder's eye beauty in fairness that is

readily conceived as admirable while the darkness of skin color is conceived as base and unattractive.

Isn't this a terrible manifestation of ignorance that is trapped in a web of societal mediocre perceptions about the dignity of one's race? Where conscience immediately feels trapped in the guilt of color bars and then tends to feel resentful toward its own very image, identity, and personality?
Yet the beauty of color lies in the "eye of the beholder."

Dramatizing the Art

The art of producing a movie is so fascinating to watch
at the Oscars in Los Angeles,
as a series of dramatic films
project on giant screens,
depicting attitudes that
reflect a hilarious *end!*

A cigarette-fuming writer
crashes a typewriter through
a glass window of a high-rise
building,
comedians pun on the iconic
word *love,*
frustration is ridiculed in multiple
twisted sheets of wasted paper, and
angers flare up on screen.
Yet, in the hiatus, I see host Ellen
lapping a manuscript to Martin Scorsese
in this crowded hall of famers as
Martin promises to read and render feedback.

Such is the pathway for future screenwriters
and careerists,
whose ambitions sprout out of insignificance,
then mature to fruition in the dramatic
selection of nominees and best award nominee,
at this seventy-sixth Oscar* and future others,
when hopefuls' dreams come true as they
parade the red carpet to the hall of fame.

So, comrades, keep the dream alive,
for you never know the hour when

---

* Date: Sunday, March 25, 2007. Event: Oscar nominations for
the year 2006 in Los Angeles.

your script will manicure its way into
the hands of a Spielberg or a Scorsese.

The secret to it all!
"Keep the dream alive!"

Today in New York City

(Snippets from the daily news)

Something so tragically eerie yet familiar happened
that sent resident New Yorkers scampering
down the streets of downtown Manhattan
in total shock, and frightful awe.

A small airplane had just struck a twenty-eight-story high-rise
building, located close to the East River,
and was dangling over the city itself.

The building immediately sparked wild scorching hot
flames about two levels on the upper side.

Firefighters and crews scrambled to extinguish the flames.
Surgeons in emergency room uniforms and other medical
personnel including the NYPD rushed to the scene, and
sealed off the area.
In the classroom teaching at that time,
I heard not of it.
Then on my way home with my two little kids,
the news radiated in the airwaves of FM 103.5.
That was bad news.

Later that evening,
the horror scene unfolded before my eyes, reminiscent
of a miniature 9/11.

Then I really became scared.
Was it another 9/11?

CNN's 360 unfolded the pilot's passion to fly planes.
A New York Yankees pitcher,
he had just become a licensed pilot in February
and could fly a plane to anywhere.

He had a wife and a son.
Instantly, I had goose bumps
just thinking about his family.
So I clutched my baby to my heart
and tears rolled down my eyes.

.

I knew you not, but I pray for you.
You lived a life too soon and died too soon.
But death can never snatch fond memories of you
from your family and loved ones who knew you.
His precious name was Cory.

I Boarded a Train

From Munich to Berlin, one warm Saturday
evening of July's summer, to visit Joanna
and Tom-Tom, and what my eyes saw
transformed my mind to vicissitudes of
imaginary novelty and beauty, read only in
paperback, in my past life of a reader less
traveled.

Peeking through the window of my
train seat in the wee hours of an early
morning,
the greenery of extensive landscapes,
formulated in alphabetic farmlands,
revealed a countryside that sharply
contrasted with that of my humble
origins.

I was struck by the view of such natural
beauty, blended with the single-family
homes that separated from each other
across vast acres of farmland, identified
in maize fields and wheat fields, interspersed
with winding suburban streets that led to
communities, populated by skilled farmers.

Then I thought about the farmers who cultivated
such expansive lands.

In contrast to my humble origins, farmlands in
Kom were cultivated by mothers and grandmothers
using hoes and cutlasses, with such farms situated
on narrow, hilly plain fields that took hours to walk to.
From Meyef, to Kindo, to Iseilah,*
no houses were located in such vicinities and

---

* Meyef and Kindo are small neighborhoods in the village of kom, in the
northwest region of Cameroon, that consist of vast expanses of farmland.

the crude method of farming rendered the
hands all blistered, red, worn, and old.
Buzzing past Nuremberg, the trials of Nuremburg
studied in history, in my high school days, revived
memories of tough world wars long fought and won,
then fought and lost in a continent of Europe, trapped
in a swift revolution of periodic industrialization.

Then, I shivered and sat up in the train.
I thought about the toil of our grandmothers
back home.
I thought about my own grandmother Anna
Veronica Bih then, and now, climbing the steep
hills of Njinikom's valleys to till with hoes and
cutlasses the hard unproductive soil that begged
to be nourished with nature's fertilizers.

A sense of trepidation invaded my thoughts at
that moment.
I stared at the blank, youthful faces on the train
who knew nothing about hoes, yet some smoked
cigarettes nonchalantly, while a few strangely wore
tiny symbolic s-bands on their arms reminding me
of wars long fought, won, and then lost.

Then, a deep sense of pride and admiration for the
coarse and blistered hands of our grandmothers that
had fed grandchildren who could venture into a daring
world of fascinating contrasts overwhelmed me as
the train shuttled on.

I drifted into an uncomfortable sleep, with the
penetrating rays of sunlight invading my silent
thoughts.
As the farmlands slowly disappeared in a haze before
my eyes, I woke up to find myself in the next
inter-regional train station, ready to board another train
to Berlin.

I Remember

Standing on the second floor
of my dad's balcony at Hypodrome,
staring at the moon and stars
shining against a cool night sky,
contemplating and yearning for
the unknown.

Remorseful feelings of despair,
reminiscent of wasted years
robbed gray with the passage
of time occupy my thoughts.

Having as most valuable asset
hundreds of credit hours served,
honored with a college degree, yet
haunted with feelings of guilt
harbored by total dependence on
hearty parents at an advanced age.

So would I grimly stare in wonder at
the starry night sky,
silently demanding all my yearnings
from the almighty one
secretly known only to him and I
solemnly, in deep prayer and contemplation.

Yet would I dare to exhibit such confidence?
In my heart?
Yielding to tempting doubts that secretly
engulf my mind
yanking a future destined by him?
Yet I dare not be a Pyrrhonist.

Here I stand today in another country,
in another continent,

having harnessed the fruits of belabored
prayers
heaving a sigh of relief as I stare out my
bedroom window on this cold, wintry night.

So it is the same universe, the same moon,
the same stars, and the same world
splendidly contrasted by putrid, aggravated
self-delusive destructiveness,
pitted against monumental, advanced, highbred,
cognitive minds
which have challenged disillusions
and bred modern democracies.

Instead of hopelessness, despair, and a
longing for the unknown,
my footing is now planted on the solid
earth.
Incessant yearnings have now yielded to
ambitious careers pursued in a rotating
world of equalities.

Who holds the key to the puzzle now?
The past or the present?

June 16, 2011

Dreams are vivid memories that surface in the conscious mind
  at the dawn of sunrise, yet loom in the deep recesses of the
  subconscious mind at sunset.

Do Not Let Go of Your Dreams

When the sun descends behind the clouds
at dusk and darkness looms overhead,
          do not let go of your dreams.

When your life spirals out of control
and you loose the things you have worked
so hard to achieve, do not let despair overcome
your fragile spirit;
do not be afraid of the unknown enemy that lurks
in the shadow of darkness;
          Do not let go of your dreams.

Your worried dreams and lost thoughts are only
the beginning of a new path traced to the origin
of your life;
For as the pendulum swings and you go round
in circles, you will once more find yourself right
where you started, at the beginning of time,
as the piercing sun shyly lights up the morning sky,
          signaling the dawn of a new day.

So, do not let go of your dreams,
    and your ambitions,
        and your hopes,
Do not let go of your dreams,
do not let misery over power your spirit,
for you are only at the beginning of life's journey,
a journey that will know no end,
          until the end of time.

Ignorance

Ignorance bred in the mind
can become a dangerous tool
for retribution.

A springboard of man's demagogic ways
devilishly manifested through vicious smiles
often nurtured in the minds of boastful pessimists.

Blurred visions of racial prejudice hidden in
dark silk suits and polished soles roaming hallways
yet symbols of power embedded in systematic
havens of authority in institutions that be.

What a waste for visionary optimists
trapped in a web of constant intimidation,
deceit, and hypocrisy, resonating from ignorant
minds that have embraced subjectivity over objectivity.

Tinted glasses have blurred their narrow
minds and tainted their limited vision of a
multifaceted world whose increasing
cultural diversity has bred a multiplicity of
wagging tongues in a stereotyped society
that often rejects acculturated English
mother tongues in the saintly name of articulate,
conservative, untarnished, and standardized
integration.

So is articulate integration not a varying
reminiscence of blended, standardized
acculturations that have bred new tongues
in a melting pot of cultures uniquely
integrated in multiple professions in
a twenty-first-century, post–Cold War era?

Why reject it?
Ignorance, rather than become a tool for
retribution,
look yourself in the mirror and read
through the looking glass, the inscriptions on the wall.
Trips, trips, trips abroad.

Thursday Morning

It is an early Thursday morning
and a very busy morning.

I drop off Brandon at school;
Then, I drop off Gabby at Dolly's.
It is rush hour and the streets of Laurel-Bowie
197 are jammed with traffic on this dull
morning as people rush to work.

There is a burnt car on the opposite side of the
street.
Police block the road from on coming traffic.
My mind is weary on this day;
With my husband just returned from burying his
dad across the ocean, the mood is still somber at home.
Yet, yesterday evening, we laughed heartily,
and viewed the ceremony of Ba James's burial on video.

So suddenly, I realize that I am getting old.
Mildred passed at summer's end;
Ba James passed at autumn's fall;
and now Frank has just sneaked past them all.

I sit on the couch and contemplate about their life.
Tears sting my eyes as I think of them all at this
moment, and ponder over their fate before the
golden gate.
Are they in?

As police clear the street in about five minutes,
I continue driving to work, wondering how my
day will turn out.
I look at my watch and the time is about 8:15a.m.
I keep driving, while listening to 95.1F.M,
my favorite morning radio station.

It has been very stressful to work there lately.
I am now trapped between two doors of deceit,
with a lone soul in the office across the hall
serving the obscure interests of the other in
plain sight.
Nothing makes sense anymore as the iron fist
slams its doors and I step back!
The experience is chilling!

On my way home from work, I think about Millie,
and the wonderful weekends we spent together
with big Tony and small Tony, when they visited us
from Virginia.
Those were the good old days indeed.

I think about Ba James sitting at Ntamfoang square
infront of his store with a happy smiling face.
I miss him already. I wonder how it will feel
like when I go home when he is no longer there!

I think about Frank, Dolly's husband, who took
great care of Brandon and Gabriel.
I think of the fun we had attending the kids' birthday
parties at Chuck E. Cheese's, or the Bowling Alley
and I smile heartily.

I think about all of them and pray silently. I pray
for their souls to rest peacefully in the lord.

All these memories cloud my mind as I park in
the drive way, open the door, and hug my kids
waiting for me in the stair well.
All at once they shout- "mommy, mommy,"
what did you bring for me today?

My last chore of the day earnestly begins and I
wind up in bed tired, waiting to see what Friday
holds for me

June 20, 2006
Barging In

Peeking down the wide, cream white balcony
of my second-floor apartment,
on a ninety-five-degree summer,
Tuesday afternoon of June 20, 2006,
My eyes suddenly focus on a gray squirrel, nosing its
mouth on the lawn of my downstairs neighbor's apartment,
hungrily searching for food on the mowed lawn.

As it continues its desperate search, dipping its
mouth into the ground and picking up the bits
and pieces, all I can think of is the dirt and the filth
as this thought consumes my mind and makes me to
contemplate on the difference between man's free but
sensitive nature,
and the carefree attitude of animals.

Then a little boy suddenly rushes by, and
the squirrel scampers off to the tree trunk
of a huge mahogany tree
overlooking my balcony to continue its
daily routine.

Wednesday, November 26, 2008
Chaotic Voices on the Dining Table

Brandon shouts to Gabriel,

"You want more, but you had four.
You want more teaspoon scoops,
but you had four teaspoon scoops.
You want more quarter teaspoon scoops of butter,
but you had a quarter more teaspoon scoops of butter.
You want more quarter teaspoon scoops of butter on your oodles of
noodles
but you had a quarter more teaspoon scoops of butter on your oodles
of noodles.
Did you hear that, baby?"

"No!" Gabriel screams and yells … at Mummy! "I want more,
Mummy!
More … more … more!"

Then mummy adds a tiny quarter teaspoon scoop of butter on his
oodles of noodles … and the tears and screaming stop abruptly! As
Brandon again screams,

"Gabriel,
You want more, but you had four!" laughing!
"You want more, but you had four!" laughing!
"You want more, but you had four!" laughing!
"You want more, but you had four scoops of butter!" laughing
over and over again.

"Cut it out, Brandon," I scream.

Then Gabriel shouts, "Stop, Brandon. Mummy says stop!"
as the eating of oodles continues in gusty, hasty, swallows of
delicious appetite.

"Gabriel, Brandon, go to your room and don't come out. You are on time-out!"
Mummy orders.

Who is out of control here?

The Flickering Candlelight

It is a new day and a rainy morning,
with the rooftop of the church almost blown
away by the loud and thunderous rainstorm
that frightens, then sends chills down the spines
of a mournful congregation, gathered for the funeral
of he that passed away on the joyful day of his
sister's wedding.

The sister, the bride, and the horror of it all
send chills down my spine as the dancing
within the tent in the compound suddenly comes
to a dramatic, screeching halt on this late
Saturday evening with the breaking of the
tragic news from the hospital:
He is gone!

So ends the celebration of joy at this hour.
Our clothes, we tear off our bodies
and jubilation turns into mourning as I have
not seen in my years growing up.
Why is death such a familiar stranger our midst
at this time?

It is a very rainy Saturday evening and we must
make it to the compound of he that passed,
as is the tradition in my village.
The rain has turned the narrow road below the
church into thick, muddy, slippery, puddles.
We glide down the narrow path in darkness
with one foot after the other, sunk deep into mud.
There is neither moon nor stars in the dark skies.
All around me is pitch darkness.
Torchlight, we have not, but eyes we have as
the vision that leads us through.

I anxiously climb the veranda of the main house
and enter the parlour.
There is a lone flickering candlelight in the shadow
of darkness that lights up the room where he lays.
My tear-filled eyes focus on the flickering light
on the high night stand and the sound of hoarse,
heavy snore-like breathing startles me.
For a moment, I almost think he is alive and breathing
 as an eerie feeling overwhelms me.
But this is real, and this is life at this moment as I live it.

In the kitchen, the moans of wailing grandmothers,
mothers, brothers, sisters and all can be head loud
and heartbreakingly painful.
They all sit squalidly on their butts on mud floors
around a three stone fire place, while others are
cramped on the bed.
They take the edges of their worn "wrappas" that have
gathered the dirt on the floors and wipe their noses and
angry tears of grief. They are inconsolable: Another lose
in the family again? When will it end?
My grim thoughts suddenly shift as I shiver and
sit up.
The terrible winds are still howling outside the
church, while mass goes on.

The priest in church solemnly continues the sermon
with whispering mutters of bad-luck and evil omen
spiraling out of control from ear to ear.
My sister and I, gripped by fear, sit still and listen
 to the zinc on the rooftop of the church howl, crash,
and bang loudly while the down pour outside floods
 the gutters and streets, as the corpse of he that passed,
 lies before the alter.

I sit still and bow my head as the sermon continues.
I can hardly hear the father's preaching now with the

loud angry winds and severe thunderstorms threatening
to wreck havoc on the church windows and walls.

Yet, it all comes to pass as he is laid to rest peacefully,
in the midst of howling winds, raging thunderstorms,
and large hailstones that beat our tired rain soaked
bodies as we exit the grounds of the still cemetery.

Today, my father lies there too and who knows what
tomorrow will look like?
Only the shadow of a flickering candlelight still clings
 to my memory on this day as the two who so wed
on this day still smile grimly at the turn of events that
turned their wedding day into a day of mourning.
They will never forget.

Perennial Woes at Crossroads

My eyes have seen the world so differently
in the wee hours of this early Sunday morning,
at this moment that I sit and perform the habitual
semester routine of correcting students' composition
scripts.

Worn out, it yet is a new day that has dawned.
At the richness of autumn's beginning, the chilly, whispering
winds and gloomy weather tighten my mood and make me
feel sleepy.

I now realize that I am at the crossroad of life's mid-journey and just
when
all begins to blossom in my eyes in a series of charted priorities
that stall my being, I sit up, shake off the weariness like a cat just
awake from a nap, and say, "It is not the end yet, for my cup is still
full of perennial woes ready to consume me, if I give up."

Lucky

Where is Dolly's cat, Mummy?
It is lying under Frank's Lexus truck
staring at you and me, Gabriel.
Then it jumps onto the roof of
Frank's truck and quietly goes to sleep.

Today, I come out of Mummy's car, and there lies
Lucky, basking under the blazing, eighty-degree
sunshine.
I run toward Lucky and ruffle his fur, as
Lucky licks his paws and rolls over on his back.
Then I say, Mummy, Lucky has a mouth, and ears,
and eyes, and a nose, and teeth, and legs, and a
tummy, … ghee …ghee … ghee, I laugh.

My Mother's Kitchen

My mother's kitchen is a brown mud brick house
with two plank windows adorning the walls,
while a polished brown door in the center leads into
the house.
At the center of the kitchen is a three stone fireplace,
with two thin bamboo beds affixed to walls that face
each other.
Above the fireplace is a "banda" where mama stores
all her seasonal harvest and delicacies.
Yet, when the smoke from the fireplace consumes
 the kitchen air, and suffocates me, I cough loudly,
yet feel relieved that it is drying the corn so we would
not go hungry at the end of the next season of dryness.

I enter the kitchen on a late Saturday evening
after a walking trip to three corners, the village
square.
The coldness of the mud floors prick my toes,
yet the welcome smell of roast corn popping and
cracking in the crackling charcoal flames of the
three stone fireplace stimulate hunger in my belly.

I grab a corn cob from the red coals with my bare
hands and hungrily bite the hot grains off the cob.

Then with my "nkem" supported by a long stick
hung on my back, I follow my cousins, sisters,
and brothers to the farm the next day.
We rush down the Kindo farm fields with speed,
and Innocent who is too young, carries one corn
in his little "Nkem" up the winding hills tiredly.

On our way home, we tell stories of our
ancestors and enjoy the wit of it all.
We meet Odili La Kfang on our way home

down by the little stream, below my grandmother's
compound when we go to drink water and run.
We are afraid to go near her because she is a mad
woman who is harmless and unpredictable yet she
is very cautious that no one invades her homeless
shelter by the stream.
We dump all the harvested corn on my mama's
kitchen floor and go more rounds till the day's
end.

That is why I enjoy sitting in my mother's kitchen
in the rainy season, telling stories with my sisters
and cousins, eating cornmeal and vegetables, and
roasting fresh corn.

That was life back in the day, when I visited my
aunt during the rainy season and stayed in the
village.
That was a part of my childhood, a childhood
which I still deeply cherish and hold dear to my
heart.

The Folly of My Desire

Is so destructive that it has consumed
my entire being and turned me into an
alcoholic.

As I drive through the streets of
Ridge Lane Commons with bloodshot
eyes and a liquor bottle in hand,
I zigzag dangerously between the lanes,
like a Nascar racer heading for a crash.

My anger and frustration immediately
spills over to road rage as in a blur,
I see two teenage boys swiftly switch
lanes, hitting the front bumper of my
Lincoln Continental, and I just keep
zigzagging between the lanes, as
they speed off.

Voicing curses in slurs and dizziness,
I watch the two kiddos U-turn into
Park Ridge High, and I chase them
furiously into the parking lot.

Overwhelmed by the incessant screams of
frightened students, overpowered by instant
security, I just pass out as the drama unfolds.

Beyond my Eyes

I saw you look into my eyes and see
beyond the me that stood before you.

Then I wondered what you saw,
for the color bar in me, as dark as my
ancestral past radiated in your brilliant
eyes, reflecting golden hues of brown
and black that traced the map of a unique
origin, lost in the eyes of laughter that
questioned my presence in your midst.

My African Heritage

I am black,
      deep black,
charcoal black,
      ebony black,
like the roots of my African heritage;
They claim that my tongue is heavy,
saying that I have a strong one.
Yet, I look them in the face and say-
my tongue is my African pride,
where I come from, from the hills and
valleys of Belo, Njinikom, and Fundong,
I am my heritage, just as you are a product
of your own rich cultural heritage.
So do not treat me different, particularly when
our roots converge where the oceans meet and
separate the two continents in stories of a past,
mangled, and hand cuffed by the ruthless evils of
a slavery that taints our past.

Better still, I am the other me;
I am my half-sister –
and
I am black,
      half black,
banana yellow black,
      orange yellow black,
chocolate brown,
like the roots of my mixed heritage.
They claim that I am not white, because I am black,
and only half white.
Yet, what they fail to understand is that a combination
of black and white is a product of my mixed heritage,
a heritage I will not renounce, since I belong to both
worlds.
So do not reject me and the identity I bear because
of the cruel deeds of a bleak past, executed by slave

masters on our own.

All you need to know is that,
 I am black,
like the roots of my African heritage
that runs in my veins.

So who are you anyway?

Part V: Politics and Relationships: A Vision of Reality that Questions Morality

"When power leads man toward arrogance,
poetry reminds him of his limitations.
When power narrows the areas of man's concern,
poetry reminds him of the richness and diversity of his experience.
When power corrupts, poetry cleanses. ... For art establishes
the basic human truths which must serve as the touchstones of our
judgement. The artist ... faithful to his personal vision of reality,
becomes the last champion of the individual mind and sensibility
against an intrusive society and an offensive state."

John F. Kennedy

Strikes

Strikes are a result of anger, frustration, and
a total loss of hope.

Its violence spills as fast as a tsunami into
streets littered with chars of human flesh,
burned to the bone, and hot, scorching smoke
spiraling into the air in thick, cloudy layers of black
tire-burned smoke, piled in heaps onto each other
like the mountains of trash that litter and consume
the putrid air of Marché Ocala and its neighboring streets.

Its victims are the tools of stratified lunatics
who have usurped ignorant democracies
built on the strings of fragile, post-colonial ideologies,
trapped in an obsessive rage of vain loyalty to obloquy
lunatics of power who have forgotten that
the flesh that bore their breathing bones are the
remnants of dust that created their being.

While some victims are bundled like sheep in military trucks,
and lashed like slaves in a Kunta Kinte episode,
amidst groans and screams, the stampede of bloody,
blistered, and captured other victims on University campuses
transform into insults, then revenge tactics inflicted
on future intellectuals by a vicious circle of
ignorant "sans gallons" littered on the
streets to execute lethal punishment on the critics
of insane power mongers, indifferent to the plight
of the very citizens who voted them into office.

Mica's heart stops beating for a minute as she sees a
barrage of ten uniformed green berets from Batanga
rushing toward her at the university junction.
Their guns point directly at her face as she hears several clicks.
Alarmed, she panics and begins to wail.

She raises her tiny arms above her head in total
surrender.
She goes on her knees, and they quickly demand her student ID.
Suddenly, Mica becomes the biblical Peter, who denied Christ
three times before the cock crowed.
"Please, do not hurt me! I am innocent."

"I did not participate in the strike so please! Let me go!
Please do not arrest me!"
She dramatizes in French, afraid to betray her Anglophone
identity.

The bloodshot, hostile eyes of one of the green berets
prey on her like a hungry lion craving human flesh.
So she begins to feverishly pray in her heart.

So suddenly, a soldier rants, *"Laissez la parti!"*
The guns click, and she falls face down on the pavement,
in dramatic, instant fright.

Alarmed, she wakes up to find herself in a police cell, surrounded
by her university female peers, arrested on campus for the
call on democracy in a polarized nation of intolerance.
What is she supposed to do now?

That is the question!

Katanga

Katanga, a land of riches
Katanga, a land of plenty
Katanga, a land of cobalt
Katanga, a land of diamonds
Katanga, a land of gold
Katanga, a land of silver.

Yet,

Katanga, a land of poverty
Katanga, a land of misery
Katanga, a land of bribery
Katanga, a land of corruption
Katanga, a land of exploitation
Katanga, a land of thievery
Katanga, a land of violent rape
if doomed to be born a woman,
Katanga, a land of brutal deaths.

Such inhuman torture, mangled on
one of their own,
with child soldiers, remnants of
children that mothers bore, yet now are
the very ones who inflict the most pain
on the hands that bore and fed them,
with no remorse, nor end in sight.

So be it that,

the Chinese supervisor
speaks neither English
nor French
to the local miners, as they
gesture and sign language
each other in a farcical comedy

of Fran-Chen's body language.
Such is the despicable plight of native miners
from within and without, trapped in
a circle of systematic, low-wage labor
for the
French,
      Chinese,
Belgian,
      Canadian,
American,
      and British supervisors.

How long will this colonial epidemic of malfunction
continue its senile existence
in Africa my homeland?

Why are we so cursed when we are so blessed?
What is wrong with the system?
Warlords who fought for the liberation are now the liberated
suckers of wealth, gold, diamonds, and the utmost propellers
of gruesome rape.

So, who is better?
The warlord?
The seasoned politician?
The opposition?
      Or the gold diggers?

Yet the powerless and speechless citizens all sit helpless and watch
as
the horror of this comic episode unfolds before their eyes.

What an irony for the name it bears!*

---

*   My inspiration to write this poem is drawn from a BBC (British Broadcast-
ing Cooperation) world report by a British journalist on July 28, 2006, whom I
listened to while driving to a doctor's appointment. He reported on the economic
plight of the war-torn West African country known as the Democratic Republic
of Congo, where exploitation, corruption, and greed had deprived (and is still
depriving) its citizens of its natural resources.

Sunday, October 29, 2006
Campaign Ads

Two teddy bears
run on a desert strip
on a cold and windy afternoon
of October 29th.

One dresses in *blue* heavyweight jersey.
The other dresses in *red* heavyweight jersey.
Then so suddenly, before I blink my eyes,
the one in red
punches the head of
the one in blue,
as the two instantly vanish into the horizontal mist,
in the midst of such comic rivalry.

Such a small ad
is but a mini-bully,
expressing the raging fury
of a political campaign
on a visual battlefield,
turned
fiercely ugly, and downright mean to the core,

in colors of *red* and *blue*.

In the Eyes of the Storm

(Barack Obama campaigning for the 2008 presidential elections)

Massive crowds of obsessed fans
storm the campaign grounds
as he stares in wonder through the
tinted windshield of the limousine,
steering toward
the arena of his historic platform oratory.

He gazes in a daze,
He watches in wonder,
He admires in amazement,
He waves emotionally,
He smiles broadly,
He stares in disbelief,

and so I say—

Is it that a man of color has changed
the course of history?

Then I ponder and wonder,
Hey, man, wake up!

The campaign is still on and rolling,
and
he is battered, and beaten down
by the hurling winds that shatter his
existence, and expose his humble
origins, traced to his Kenyan fatherland
in live TV images of non-fictional reality.

He is torn, then ripped apart,
by a media that shows neither
mercy nor sympathy for a campaign,

run on the highs and lows of
his fascinating oratories,
charismatic personality, and
as he tirelessly navigates
multiple campaign grounds across cities
in the United States,
he is under scrutiny for his religious
affiliations ... torn apart by hate speeches,
betrayal of country, and an allegiance pledge:
honored or not honored?
That is the question again!

Yet,
he is a symbol of light that has
generated a glimmer of hope
in the chaos of a massive economic catastrophe
which, like a volcano, has exploded and
melted down—Wall Street,
auto industries,
giant companies,
and a host of others,
all demanding government bailouts,
as the darkness that surrounds him has now
transformed into a euphoric worldwide
scenario fit for a Hollywood movie production,
for that will be it.

He now stands on the pedestal of
public scrutiny as
talk show hosts and career journalists
whose stormy debates hypnotize his eyes
invade the screen, and battle the pirates
of manipulation who seek his downfall.
So is there any wishful thinking here?
For he can only weather the storm
in the eyes of the storm.

The Gallows

Fear not,
_____, my brothers,
For I have lived my life and
it is now over._____

A humble, powerless man I am,
as I head to the gallows,
with the demonic word
"hatred,"
a grim reminder of my brutal,
yet vindictive past, as
it be the last word broadcast worldwide
to my people--------
and my family; now refugees
in their once sumptuous, golden palaces,
built on the rocky surroundings of
thatched huts, and beggars.

Powerless I am in my cell,
with destructive emotional
anger having subsided,
through years of intense meditation
in my solitude as I have U-turned
to my God and Master and
suddenly yearned for him with an
intense passion that renders me oblivious to
my immediate surroundings,
and transported me to his kingdom
in my haunted dreams.

So I repent and beg for
"forgiveness,"
dear brothers, whom I have
killed in torture chambers,
destroyed, and hurt their families,

before I head to the gallows;
as with deep regret, I now suddenly
realize the mortal, yet fatal consequence of
my actions in my years of absolute
control and power.

For now that my crown and sons are captured,
destroyed, and shattered to pieces,
the scales in my eyes have fallen,
though I have failed to capture the lunatic pirates
who hijacked my memory these long years.
But,
I, too, am a shattered man inside as
everyday I weep, hurt, and babble
in solitary confinement.

Yet, my sole confidence and consolation
lies in my newly discovered greatest treasure,
previously misused, abused, and tarnished
but,
treasured, revered, and worshipped now
with a total surrender of my physical self,
that will soon become immaterial and ashy
dust, returned to the very earth,
that I once prowled like an angry lion,
devouring my enemies unscrupulously
and viciously through horrendous,
obscene actions masterminded
by pros.

But I tell you something brothers …
Revenge not …
Swear not …
Hate not … Chastise not …
And …
Cherish your valuable freedom …
Let love for mankind …

a model character to be emulated ...
humility of self ...
forgiveness of others ...
and a good interpretation of the word of God
pattern the remainder of your days,
in this life,
as I, a humble and powerless man now,
with my eyes not blindfolded but
hands and feet shackled, head
to the dreary gallows ...

But beware, brothers,
For revenge is not the solution
to the problem, but the cause,
because
the forces of the insurgency will
defeat the peace, and the war like a
wildfire in the California mountains
will rage on ...
on
the bloody streets of Baghdad.

So why
"revenge?"

Transgressions of a Corrupt Guard

It is the end of the month, and salary vouchers from
the ministry of finance are out. I rush to the bank to cash
my paycheck.

I get stuck in traffic and hear the angry blast of cabdrivers in
yellow taxis screaming angrily at the top of their voices.
What am I thinking anyway? It is midday in Yaoundé,
and I am in the heart of the city where street vendors,
burglars, and regular pedestrians prowl the streets in
in a haste and in a daze.

I get angry and frustrated because I need to enter
the bank without any hassle and get some money.
Customers are lined in single file in front of the bank
with desperate, needy looks plastered on their weary, hungry faces.
There is a sudden stampede as the line gets longer and
narrows into the street, creating that commotion of a
traffic jam, which sets cabdrivers furious.

Then the usual bank guard, who is dark, short, stout, and
aggressive, instantly moves to the bank door, very alert.
Wearing a coffee-brown, short-sleeved khaki uniform,
with his shoulders raised high, he has this fake, angry look
on his face similar to that of a police officer checking the
car documents of a cabdriver on the roadside with ulterior
motives in mind, typical in this setup.
I suddenly feel disgusted with the whole scenario as I bite
my tongue in frustration.

Then, on a signal from his mobile phone, the guard frantically
moves to the bank door, unhooks, and fiercely pushes the
iron bar at the entrance to let a set of customers out of the bank,
but the unruly crowd surges forward, and a wild stampede ensues.
He roughly pushes and angrily curses at the crowd in loud blurts of
words stringed in French clichés;

"Va la bas; fou moi le kang, est que je travail pour toi? Imbecile, kong …"

I get tossed to the side as another customer immediately usurps
my position on the line. I plead to get back in my space in vain, so I
have to start all over again. My fury, sadness, and frustration at this
moment is beyond verbal explanation.
But I must cash my money today, because I desperately need it.

Then I notice an unusual pattern of illicit activity transpiring
        between
impatient customers who cannot file up and the stout bank guard.
He sneaks customers into the side door of the bank and receives a
        bribe
ranging from five hundred to a thousand francs. These customers
        are
then led to the upper floor of the bank where their paychecks are
instantly cashed in no time. Such is the routine of the stout bank
guard who has been living off customers' paychecks to add to his.

Yet the amazing thing about such illegal transgressions by a bank
        guard
besides others is the pretence and seriousness to be performing a
        job by
rudely pushing and shoving aside respectable civil servants whose
only crime is the desire and dire need to earn their month's worth
        of labor.

Such is the characteristic of a bank guard emboldened by a
        hardcore
system of unaccountability in a corrupt system where the richest
in society are the most corrupt and the impoverished
are the most hardworking.

Who do you blame for the mess?

Die Like a Soldier

Brother, do not die like a suicide bomber
who has betrayed his own flesh and blood and
that of his fellow countrymen because of coarse
rippling voices drumming in a head that has turned
him into a brainwashed, treacherous lunatic at dawn.

For when you die with cruel objects strapped to
your own very flesh and blood which is a temple
of the holy spirit, you betray the very creator who
created this flesh and bones from the bloody dust
splashed from your rejected body and those of the
innocent souls whom you have murdered in this
ideological war of deadly proportions, hatched by
cowardly plotters, living in underground cells terrified
themselves of the very deaths that they mastermind and
execute on others.

So when you are hailed as a martyr by your fellow mentors,
know that you will be rejected and scorned by the multitude who
recognize the absurdity that there is no glorification of
lost souls in the afterlife where the choice of good and
evil prevails in a thoughtful mind that breathes life.

For after death, who knows where your soul will linger
and pursue doom's day parading the night in unearthly
ghostlike apparitions while the world sleeps, and your
mentors plot new attacks to sacrifice more human flesh?

Therefore,
in the battlefields of an illusive war, die like a patriotic soldier
who has been to the frontlines of Bagdad, Kirkuk, Peshawar,
Kabul, and Tora Bora.

Die like a soldier who has redeployed multiple times to serve his
fellow countrymen and nation, true to the spirit of his ancestors.

Prayer at the Tomb of the Unknown Soldier

There you lie in peace,
as silent as the graveyard;
Yet I know you not, and you know me not,
For you were gone, just when I migrated here,
on that fateful day at the battle of Tora Bora.

But you I see in your tombstone, as engraved on it,
are the wordings of your beloved wife Julia who missed you,
and shed rainy tears that had no end, till her dying day.

And here I stand, a stranger from afar; from across continents
that span the Atlantic Ocean and brush into the deep forests of
Africa's heartland, a heartland so unlike Conrad's in
Heart of Darkness.

Yet, you won't believe who I saw today,
When I visited Arlington Memorial,
where I saw the tombstone of an unknown soldier,
and shed a tear and two, for he looked so dashingly handsome
in his green beret, paying allegiance to the flag of the
United States of America.

So what I will remember of you, dear soldier, is that dimpled smile,
that dents into your cheeks, as you are vividly remembered as a
man who honorably served his country, and died honorably,
defending it at the battle field.

For you I see today, and I pray earnestly that your soul
will rest in perfect peace.

A Soldier in Agony

He went to the war front at Kabuli a sane man;
He returned from the war front at Kabuli a mad man.
When he talked, he made no sense to all.
The war had battered, and shattered him physically,
and mentally.
He had bits of shrapnel still buried in his left leg.

Then one day, he ran out of his house naked in broad daylight.
He hit the streets of the city close to the National Assembly
building at noon, under the sweltering heat, when civil servants
were heading home for lunch.
All eyes stared in shock and bewilderment.
Was he crazy? Yes he was.
What drove him crazy?

He was married with four kids.
He was cramped in a two bedroom complex at a Military
Barracks with his family.
His wife's name was Lucia, and she was a struggling,
uneducated, housewife.
He had gone to the village of Abula ten years ago and
married her.

At this moment, his wife was saddled with a deep sense of grief,
and trepidation.
She abandoned her kids at home, and chased her husband down
the street as he ran, while wailing, and mourning …
Then she tripped on her flip flops, and fell heavily on the ground,
as her "wrappa" broke loose around her waist.
She quickly pulled the "wrappa" around her waist, brushed the
sand that had bruised her bloody knees with her fingers, and
kept on running steadily …..

Then others joined her, and he was soon caught.
He was sweating profusely, and breathing heavily.

The crowd lay him on the ground to rest, and went their way,
for there was no ambulance to take him to the hospital,
nor 911 to call for immediate help.
No taxi would carry him for his wife had no money to pay a
taxi cab.

It was a different country and a different world, yet it was
Lucia's country, and Lucia's world of crushed dreams.

That was the reality of Lucia's world, since her husband returned
from the war front, and this was the reality that faced Lucia now;
 Her husband, or her kids?
She was very confused.

He would not seek medical help, because he thought that;
he was a man,
        a real man,
a strong man,
        and a full blooded African man,
with a pride of his own,
        too proud for others to see his pain.
He kept eloping from the mental institution where he was
 hospitalized;
The reason why he was at home on this day!

He had returned from the warfront a disgruntled, a confused,
and an angry man.
He needed money to keep his family going, but his pay was
too low to make ends meet.
When he talked to his superiors, they waved him off, and
dismissed him from their presence.
Yet, he had received three medals of honor for a brilliant
military service to his nation, when the war at Kabuli
raged on;
                ---------- a medal for sustaining wounds at the battle front,
                ---------- a medal for his bravery in killing the enemy at
                        the battle front,

---------- and another, for saving the life of a wounded
soldier on the battle field.

So standing on the sidewalk of the national assembly building,
his wife, with the help of a kind stranger stopped a taxi, took her
husband home, and continued with her perennial woes,
tired of walking the halls of mental institutions that changed
nothing in her husband's condition.

This was her story, and this was his story.
Will he accept medical treatment in the end?

However, as broke as he is, he is so proud to have served
his country at the battle field of Kabuli.
As he runs out into the street the next day, he has on his
shoulders, three medals of honor glittering like gold in the
sunshine.
He is wearing green khaki military uniform, and whistling
to himself, while he crosses the street to enter the military
barracks.
His green beret is neatly folded and put in the back pocket
of his green khaki pants.
The guard at the gate gives him a military salute, and he responds
with laughter, and a straight bow of his head, responding to the
greeting accordingly.

How will today look like for him?
All I know is that he is a soldier in agony who returned
from the war front a mad man, struggling to find his way
in a corrupt system.

Yet, dare I criticize the system and blame it for the burden
that has devastated the world of a soldier, his wife Lucia,
and their kids?

What system is in place, to carter for the needs of soldiers who
 return from the war front -
battered,
        wounded,
and mentally deranged?

Does anyone really care?

If they do, then let them take a close look at a mentally
unstable soldier, whose agony is trapped in a whirlwind
of dust, spiraling in the air.

The Course of History

As a recent graduate of the University of
Yaoundé, I contemplate my fate in life and
uneasily bite my tongue.

I suddenly realize that my fate is determined
not by the course of history, but by a need to
achieve my goals in life, if I decide to make a
move right now.

Yet,
how can such determination yield success when this
course serves as a deterrent to the basic condition
of human life lived in the slums and ghettos of cities
that harbor marble and gold structures?

How can the course of history be attainable when
the streets of Yaoundé and its environs are littered
with piles of dumped trash that stink in the whole
city like dead fish?

How can the course of history be attainable when
the streets of Marché Mokolo, piled high with dumps
of trash, serve as an open market for the inhabitants
that it serves?

How can it be when the "bayam-sellam" traders that it
serves sit in open stalls and dirt floors covered in tattered
cardboards to sell the very food that we cook and eat;
yet the city mayors do nothing to improve the plight of
mankind, since the politics of the belly is more enticing
than the plight of the oppressed.

How can this be when the government that should cater
to the interest of the people it has sworn to govern is
plagued with bottlenecks and a governing bureaucracy

that can intimidate others with their "voodoo" powers
at any cost to stay in a stale politics that has declined in
policy, speeches, and actionable intelligence?

How can this be when the voice of the people is
drowned in a quagmire of regional, biased policies
that profit none in the infrastructural development
of cities, and villages mangled in a web of manipulative
fraud with contractors who siphon billions from
government accounts with no accountability and
no projects? So the roads remain the same or develop
massive potholes one year after that litter muddy rain
water on innocent pedestrians like us who are not
responsible for the chaos.

Yet, our voices are drowned in all this cacophony of
wasted years that render us permanent beggars at
the IMF, piled with high interest rates that can pay
millions of workers in a month.

Who do you blame for all this stagnant waste, exploitation,
and abuse of democracy that has rendered my home
country poverty-stricken
and full of wrath with oppressive policies that the colonizers
imposed on this part of our hemisphere?

What a tragedy that several years after
independence, we are still caught in the very traumas
that our ancestors were responsible for in the trade of
African slaves from the shores to the West because of
our greedy conspiracy to attain wealth.

So when do we move on when the future is still so bleak and
holds no promise of change?

What can I do for my country when I am just a tiny little voice
in the closet straining to be heard?

Can I change the course of history, or will I someday
continue to be one amongst the brain drains that
stray back to the colonizer to seek greener pasture if
opportunity knocks?

With tears in my eyes, I weep for my country.
I feel so sad on this day, and I really wonder if there is
any hierarchy above who cares to listen to the voice of a
people it has trampled upon, abused, snubbed, and
dumped in the trash like the abandoned litters on the
streets of Marché Mokolo.

Yet, I stand here today as a graduate of the Yaoundé University,
and all I do every day to earn a living is sell "Frippery" at Marché
Mokolo."

Yet again, the course of history may seek to liberate me from
my current woes, if I choose to wrestle with the demons of my
patriotism that warn me not to be like the others who have
abandoned the system with little or no fistfight and are now
enjoying the economic benefits of overseas opportunities
abroad, which is the latest trend in third-world migration.

Or, the course of history may demand that I play the game of
politics the way it is and achieve the goals that I so yearn for
in life by blending into the fold, if "voodoo" does not eliminate
me before I achieve that goal.
But will I dare to betray the very criticism that I have voiced out
for the oppressed?

This is the choice that I now face in my country of birth;
so, which path should I follow?

Abikjan

These are the children that I know;
These are the faces that I see when
I wake up in the morning;
black, strong, masculine and sweaty faces,
struggling to survive in a war-torn city, rubbled
by the dust of stray bullets on bloody streets;
abandoned bodies lying on the tarmac and sidewalks,
and fleeing women, with children on their backs
and large straw bags on their "wrappa" bundled hair
rushing out of the city terrified, as the explosive gunshots
fade in the distance.

They flee in numbers and walk at a fast pace,
stumbling into each other's hasty feet, falling,
then rising quickly to continue the mortal journey of exile.
Will they ever return home?
This is so, so, so, so, so sad.

Yet, the lunatic stays on, rambling words of victory
on election night, when citizens are dying like sprayed flies
on the filthy streets littered with stinky garbage from which
humans and dogs feed.

I am ashamed of this type of delusional history that continues
to defy all the odds, while the voices of the poor and desperate
sink deeper into the rubble of collapsed buildings, and desperate
protesters and crying babies know not what is going on.

But history is a game changer,
since
the children of today are the builders of tomorrow,
as I feel their pain and recall how,
        these are the children that I know,
        the faces that I see,
        the strong muscled men wrought with grief,

but sweating to evacuate their families, and take them to safety.
    These are the mothers that I see,
    these are the children that I remember,
    these are the children that I know, that I love,
and now tears fill my eyes to see them suffer, because I remember
how I used to wash them when they were babies, and feed them,
and cuddle them on my mother's breast and mine.
Oh, I regret.

Yet, the* soldiers are dangerous, deadly, and armed.
They are all over the streets, in neighborhoods, and
in compounds, raping, killing, and abandoning corpses
and carcasses, while the armed militia lurks in the dark,
returning gunfire for gunfire, as the madness continues.

When will it be over?

---

*   My inspiration to write this poem is drawn from images seen on BBC America TV on March 22, 2011. Laurent Gbabgo had lost the presidential elections in Ivory Coast on November 2010. He refused to cede power to his rival Alassane Quattara who had won the elections.

Exit Point

Close to the eve of Christmas,
I sit on my home computer at Russett, idly browsing through
  pages on my husband's Face book, while smiling at the
  pictures of friends not seen for the last ten years.

Lost in thought, I ponder over my life, and its puzzling twists
  and turns.
My eyes suddenly light up and I heave a melancholic sigh
of relief.
As dreadful images of an unholy hour jolt my memory,
I realize that I am at an exit point, a transition from a world
of blackmail; hypocrisy; vanity; vengeance; and bitterness;
to a world of peaceful bliss.

Yet, who am I?
Does anyone know me better than I know myself?
Or is it just crude politics smeared by dust from narrow
  hallways that blur the vision of three lone figures charting
their paths through history in hidden corners of conference
  rooms and offices at winter's dusk when all are gone for
the day?

As I struggle to refocus my thoughts, the mouse slips
from my right palm and dangles from the desk, swinging
back and forth in quick motions that gradually slow to a halt.
In a synchronized act of self-realization, my thoughts sway,
and I rock on the seat back and forth, lost again in thought.

Like a patrol soldier at the mercy of an elusive terrorist in
  Kabul,
I am battered and caged out.
My voice is drowned in a cup of strong, addictive coffee,
sipped to the last dreg.
It is a vicious twosome circle that plots and executes randomly

to satisfy an inflated ego that manipulates and defies authority
in the face, even giggling cynically at their own follies!

What a horrible experience!
I stare in shock at the dark figure across the silent room, and my
blood runs cold.
Such arrogance electrified in the dark pitches of mocking,
boastful eyes mirrored in the dimness!
It is a very shocking experience indeed!
I become perturbed and petrified to see such an evil
countenance.
Then, I shiver and sit up, overwhelmed by intense emotion.

As I begin to promptly tap on the key board, my thoughts
embark on a journey of self-contemplation in these lines:

Wisdom lies in a mind that promotes objective rather
than subjective criticism;
A mind that is open to dialogue rather than vain intimidation;
However, a mind plagued by obscure insecurities that torture
the soul day and night, lacks a good sense of rational judgment.
So, rather than plot good deeds that will promote the
advancement of human knowledge, it selfishly plots evil deeds.

What a pity that power so obtained can be used so ungodly
in the name of moving things forward, when there is within,
such incompetence that can ruin a generation of fresh minds,
struggling to fit in a millennial jackpot of academics and
socialized networking.

Lips are sealed out of respect and not dumbness,
So when harassed, threatened, humiliated, and verbally
abused, the question that arises is: are there any laws that
protect us from such intense abuse by novices in positions
of authority who consciously violate the very laws that they
criticize?

Mindful that my destiny is controlled by God, and not by man,
I exit the stage with a sigh of relief.

_____Lessons learned, wisdom is a golden gift, found only in
golden hearts, that plot no evil day and night to destroy
others for selfish, political, self-aggrandizement.

_____So too, truth is inherently a basic part of human
nature,
so human that we may try to code lies or portray others
as evil,
we may try to use blackmail as a weapon to get even,
but the truth will always surface like a scripted reality TV
show off stage in threatening hallways and elsewhere!

_____ This too, is politics littered in the hallways
and closed doors of power obsessed hypocrites, hunched
on computers struggling to hold on to a delicate seaweed
that sways back and forth on the corals, as the waves
crash on the dark, rocky, ocean banks, blurring the vision
of the onlooker.

The onlooker pretends not to know what is going
on even on the last day when the game is over and
everyone is gone. Yet, the hallway dancers gamble
with her credibility under her watchful eyes, to take
leave of absence soon after, commending themselves
for a job well done!

The onlooker again curiously watches silently in
the background, aware of the political tactics and
mind games that have polluted an environment
riddled with secrets and un-intellectual plots
behind closed doors; Something that has absolutely
nothing to do with the growth of young intellectual
minds yearning for knowledge like a thirsty camel

in the desert.

So, is reverse psychology simply a means to an end?
or an end in itself?
That is the question!

Figures that are so _____
power hungry,
                polarizing,
 hypocritical,
            vindictive,
 deceitful,
spiteful of others,
and
presumptuous,
need to wake up and realize that
the world is fast changing, and the likes of them
will no longer be there as time progresses, and the
wheels of the gyre spin out of control, to expose severe
hypocritical tendencies and malicious plots.

However, no regrets! – Just relieved!
Just fond memories of a chapter in my past, deeply
engraved in my memory, as I remember the good old days
when it was fun to be together at the Olive Garden for lunch
eating delicious meals, chatting about the work we do,
and sharing beautiful Christmas cards.

A Vision in the Stormy Sea

I saw a shadow in a vision that flickered like a candle light
in the darkness of a dark stormy night.
A dragon that had four golden horns spitting fire into the raging
seas hastily pursued the shadow as it ran to seek refuge.

The vision spread into the tumultuous sea and anxiously
rushed against rough tides that splashed furiously against
the rocky banks, then disappeared into the stillness of the night.

I raised my eyes beyond the flickering candle light
and blinked.

My entire life, lived over a span of decades over there and here,
flickered before my eyes and danced in the candle-lit flames,
reminding me of years that had narrowed into months,
weeks, days, hours, and minutes. I was stunned.
When had time gone by so fast?

My whole life became a shadow in a vision that blurred
into the darkness that consumed the stormy sea,
transitioning from the past to the present,
where I lay, staring at the vision in my mind's eye
that flickered like a candle light in the dimness
of a dark stormy night.

Thoughts of my family consumed my spirit, consoled me,
strengthened my resolve , and gave me such peace of mind
as I had not felt in years.
In a word of prayer, I was very grateful to the Lord, in whom
I sought refuge.

I heaved a sigh of relief and this time, I waited for
an angelic voice in a vision of light to chase the shadow
of the dragon over the candle-lit flame with an alleluia song,
as the pitch of the voice roared over the tumultuous seas, rising tides,
and crashing waves to settle faintly, yet distantly, on the rooftop of a grey lighthouse that dimed into the stillness of the night.

Works Cited

Fonlon, Benard Nsokika. *Genuine Intellectuals. Academics and Social Responsibilities of Universities in Africa.* Mankon, Bamenda: Langaa Research & Publishing Common Initiative Group, 2009.

Holy Bible. Trans. Flynn, Daniel V. et al. New York,/China, 1992. New American Bible.

Tennyson, Alfred L. "Crossing the Bar." *SparkNotes.* Barnes and Nobles, n.d. Web. May 31, 2011.

Wallace, Robert, and Boisseau Michelle. *Writing Poems.* 4th ed. United States of America: HarperCollins, 1996.

Works Consulted

Carson, Anne. *The Beauty of the Husband.* United States of America: Vintage Books, 2001.